KEEP MORE CASH

How Women Entrepreneurs Write Off Their Success,

Take Control of Their Money, and Build Financial Freedom

SHEENA JONES, CPA

Founder, Growth Advisors & Tax Consultants/

She Builds Wealthy Co

Creator of the F.R.E.E.D.O.M. Framework

KEEP MORE CASH

The F.R.E.E.D.O.M. Framework

for Women Entrepreneurs

How Women Entrepreneurs Write Off Their Success,

Take Control of Their Money, and Build Financial Freedom

SHEENA JONES, CPA

ImpactMaker
PUBLISHING

Published by:

Impact Maker Publishing

Paperback ISBN: 979-8-950701-08-5

Hardcover ISBN: 979-8-950701-07-8

Digital ISBN: 979-8-950701-09-2

Disclaimer

Every effort has been made to verify the information provided in this book and its related materials. However, neither the author nor Impact Maker Publishing assumes responsibility for errors, inaccuracies, or omissions, or for any financial loss resulting from its use. Any references to people or organizations are unintentional. For legal, financial, or accounting matters, seek the services of a qualified professional. This book and related training materials are for educational and informational purposes only and are not intended as legal, financial, or accounting advice.

Earnings & Income Disclaimer

Impact Maker Publishing and its partners, affiliates, consultants, and presenters make no guarantees or claims regarding income, earnings, or results. Outcomes vary based on individual effort, skill, and application. Testimonials are individual experiences and not representative of average or typical results.

Readers and participants should exercise caution and seek professional advice before acting on any information. By engaging with this content, you agree that Impact Maker Publishing and its representatives are not liable for any direct, indirect, or consequential damages arising from the use or misuse of this book, materials, or training. All materials are provided as is, without warranties of any kind.

Examples, stories, and strategies shared are for illustrative purposes only and should not be interpreted as promises or guarantees of performance or results.

The character of Emma is a fictional composite inspired by the experiences of real women entrepreneurs. Any resemblance to a specific individual is coincidental.

First Edition, 2026

Printed in the United States of America

Table of Contents

Dedication 1

A Letter to the Reader 3

How to Use This Book 7

Meet Emma: Your Guide Through the Journey 11

CHAPTER 1 *Fortify Your Foundation* 15

CHAPTER 2 *Reduce Your Lifetime Tax Bill* 31

CHAPTER 3 *Expand Your Wealth* 49

CHAPTER 4 *Elevate Your Lifestyle* 65

CHAPTER 5 *Design Your Legacy* 81

CHAPTER 6 *Optimize Your Operations* 97

CHAPTER 7 *Multiply Your Money and Momentum* 113

Acknowledgments 127

About the Author 129

Connect with Sheena 131

Recommended Resources 133

Work with Sheena 137

Stay Connected 139

YOUR NEXT STEP 141

Dedication

This book is more than a guide; it is my legacy, dedicated to the woman who built mine.

To my mother: For years, I watched you serve as the silent rock that held our family together. I grew up determined to never depend on anyone, driven by a misunderstood version of your story. Today, I see the truth. You were not dependent; you were the unstoppable force behind our survival.

While my father could not hold a job, you held everything else. You did the work of two parents to fortify our foundation, ensuring my brothers and I had the stability you were denied. Your resilience is the primary asset that allowed me to expand my wealth and multiply my money, but more importantly, it taught me how to design a legacy of true independence.

Everything I am, and everything I teach, is a dividend of your strength. Thank you for showing me that a solid foundation is built on grit, not just gold.

For every woman entrepreneur who has ever whispered to herself in the dark, "Where is all the money I worked so hard for?" This book is your answer. This framework is your foundation. And this is your season to keep more.

A Letter to the Reader

Dear Reader,

I need to tell you something before we begin, and I need you to hear it clearly.

You are not bad with money.

You are not behind. You are not broken. You are not the only one sitting at a kitchen table at midnight, staring at numbers that do not make sense, wondering how you can earn this much and still feel this stuck.

I know that feeling. I have lived it.

I grew up watching my mother run a daycare out of our living room. She worked from sunup to sundown, feeding other people's children, holding our family together with grit and prayer while instability swirled around us. I learned early that money was something you worked for endlessly, something that never stayed long enough to feel safe, and something that always seemed to belong to someone else.

That programming followed me into adulthood. I earned the degrees. I climbed the ladder at a Big 4 accounting firm in Chicago. I wore the suits. I built the career. I invested in real estate, had a couple of very successful flips and several successful rentals as well. We did the underwriting; we came up with a *plan,* but then we trusted a crook who scammed us, and we nearly lost everything.

We survived it. Not easily, and not untouched. That season tested our savings, our confidence, and our marriage, and I will not pretend the outcome was ever guaranteed. But we stood in the wreckage together, and standing there, I had a choice. I could crawl back into survival mode, or I could rebuild with a foundation that nothing could ever shake again. No crook. No crisis. No season of loss.

I chose the foundation. And my husband chose it with me.

What I built from that season of loss became the F.R.E.E.D.O.M. Framework. It is the system I wish someone had handed me twenty years ago. Not a budgeting template. Not a motivational speech. A real, structured, emotionally honest path from financial confusion to financial confidence.

This book is that path in your hands.

I wrote it for the woman who has built something remarkable but feels like she is standing on a trapdoor. For the woman who is tired of tax season feeling like punishment for her own progress. For the woman who knows she was made for more but cannot figure out why the money keeps disappearing.

Inside these pages, you will meet Emma. She is not one woman. She is every woman I have coached, every client who has sat across from me with tears in her eyes and fire in her belly. Her story will feel familiar because it is your story told with a different name.

You will also find real strategies. Not a theory. Not platitudes. Actual tools, checklists, worksheets, and scripts that you can use the same week you read them. This is a field guide, not a feel-good book. It is designed to be used, marked up, dog-eared, and revisited every quarter.

But more than anything, I wrote this book to give you permission. Permission to look at your numbers without shame. Permission to keep more of what you earn without guilt. Permission to build wealth that feels as good in your body as it looks on paper.

You have worked hard enough to deserve clarity. Let this be the season you finally receive it.

With calm, clear power,

Sheena Jones, CPA

Founder, Growth Advisors & Tax Consultants

She Builds Wealthy Co

Creator of the F.R.E.E.D.O.M. Framework

How to Use This Book

This is not a book you read once and place on a shelf. It is a field guide. It was designed to be opened, worked through, and returned to as your business grows and your financial life evolves.

Here is how to get the most from it.

Read It in Order the First Time

The seven chapters follow the F.R.E.E.D.O.M. Framework in sequence. Each pillar builds on the one before it. Fortifying your foundation comes before reducing your tax bill for a reason. Expanding your wealth comes before elevating your lifestyle for a reason. Trust the order. The progression is intentional.

Follow Emma's Story

Every chapter opens with Emma, a fictional composite character based on the actual experiences of hundreds of women entrepreneurs I have worked with over the past eighteen years. Her story is the emotional thread of this book. She will struggle with the same fears you carry. She will ask the same questions you have been afraid to say out loud. And she will find her way through, one pillar at a time.

You are not just reading her story. You are seeing your own.

Use the Tools

Each chapter includes a checklist, a named worksheet, and at least one script or template. These are not decorative. They are the operational heart of this guide. Print them. Fill them out. Share them with your accountant, your bookkeeper, or your business partner. The women who get results from this book are the ones who pick up the pen.

Return to It Quarterly

Your business changes. Your income shifts. Tax laws evolve. I recommend revisiting one chapter per quarter and running through the checklist again with fresh eyes. What was true for you in January may look different by July. This book is built to grow with you.

Mark It Up

Highlight what hits you. Circle what confuses you. Write your own notes in the margins. Fold the corners of the pages that matter most. A clean field guide is an unused field guide. Make this one yours.

YOUR FREE F.R.E.E.D.O.M. TOOLKIT

Download the digital, fillable versions of every worksheet in this book before you begin.

shebuildswealthy.com/toolkit

Meet Emma: Your Guide Through the Journey

Emma is a woman you probably already know.

She is the friend who always looks like she has it all together. The entrepreneur whose social media tells a story of growth, momentum, and wins. The business owner who crossed six figures and felt, for one fleeting moment, like she had finally made it.

But behind the scenes, Emma is drowning.

She is a wife and a mother of two—her daughter Lily and her son Caleb. Her tax bill arrived last April and nearly broke her. Not because she was careless, but because no one had ever taught her to plan for it. She had a bookkeeper, sure, but no strategy. She had an LLC, but she did not know why. She had revenue, but she could not explain where most of it went.

Emma is smart. She is capable. She is resourceful. And she is exhausted from trying to figure out the financial side of her business alone.

She is also fictional.

Emma is a composite character. She is built from the authentic experiences, genuine fears, and real breakthroughs of hundreds of women entrepreneurs I have worked with over the past eighteen years as a CPA and business financial strategist. She is also built, in more places than you might expect, from my story. I have been the woman at the kitchen table. I have been the woman who knew better and still could not bring herself to look. The framework in this book did not come from theory. It came from lived experience on both sides of the desk.

Emma's name is made up, but her story is as real as it gets. And some of it is mine.

In every chapter of this book, you will walk alongside Emma as she encounters each pillar of the F.R.E.E.D.O.M. Framework. You will watch her struggle with the same confusion you may carry right now. You will see her ask the questions you have been too afraid to voice. And you will witness her transformation, one clear decision at a time.

Emma is not perfect. She does not get it right on the first try. She resists. She doubts. She makes mistakes. That is what makes her useful. She is not here to impress you. She is here to show you that the path from chaos to clarity is walkable, even when it feels impossible.

By the end of this book, Emma will have fortified her foundation, reduced her tax burden, expanded her wealth, elevated her lifestyle, designed her legacy, optimized her operations, and multiplied her money and momentum.

She will not be the same woman who started. And neither will you.

The F.R.E.E.D.O.M. Framework at a Glance

Pillar	Chapter Title	What You Will Build
F	**Fortify Your Foundation**	Build safety, clarity, and confidence into your financial life.
R	**Reduce Your Lifetime Tax Bill**	Stop overpaying and start planning your taxes with strategy, not stress.
E	**Expand Your Wealth**	Shift from earning income to building assets that grow without you.
E	**Elevate Your Lifestyle**	Align your money with your values and give yourself permission to enjoy what you have.
D	**Design Your Legacy**	Create intention, infrastructure, and clarity that outlives your calendar.
O	**Optimize Your Operations**	Build systems that free your time, protect your energy, and scale your business.
M	**Multiply Your Money and Momentum**	Reinvest with purpose and build compounding wealth that works while you sleep.

"You do not need to earn more to feel free. You need to keep more of what you already earn."

Sheena Jones

CHAPTER 1
Fortify Your Foundation

F.R.E.E.D.O.M. Pillar One

Build safety, clarity, and confidence into your financial life.

There is a particular kind of loneliness that comes with financial confusion.

It is not the loneliness of being alone in a room. It is the loneliness of being surrounded by people who assume you have it all figured out, while the truth sits in your chest like a stone you cannot swallow.

You have clients who trust you. A team that depends on you. A family that looks at you and sees the one who holds it all together. And yet, when you open your bank account at midnight, after everyone else is asleep, the number staring back at you does not match the effort you have poured into your life.

You are not careless. You are not reckless. You are not the woman who blows money on things she does not need. You are the woman who works harder than anyone in the room and still cannot explain where all the money goes.

That is not a character flaw. That is a foundation problem.

And you are not alone in it.

Here is the truth that will set you free, if you let it: most financial chaos is not caused by bad behavior. It is caused by an unclear structure.

You do not have a spending problem. You have a visibility problem. When your money has no home, no obvious job, and no system directing its movement, confusion is not a possibility. It is a certainty.

Clarity is not something you earn after you reach a certain revenue number. Clarity is the foundation you pour before you build anything else. Without it, every dollar you earn lands in a pile with no purpose. With it, every dollar becomes a decision you can trust.

This chapter is about building that foundation. Not with shame. Not with spreadsheets that make you feel stupid. With safety, simplicity, and a structure that finally makes your money make sense.

Emma's Story: The Night She Opened the Drawer

Emma sat cross-legged on her bedroom floor at eleven o'clock on a Tuesday night, a teetering stack of envelopes surrounding her like a paper fortress.

Bills. Bank statements. An unopened IRS notice that had been sitting in the kitchen junk drawer for three weeks. Somewhere underneath the pile was her daughter Lily's permission slip for the school field trip, due in the morning, and a birthday party invitation her son Caleb had asked about twice. The QuickBooks tab on her laptop had been open for a month, blinking like an accusation she could not bring herself to face.

"I'll deal with it tomorrow," she had whispered to herself. She had been whispering that same sentence every night for six months.

The truth was, Emma was not lazy. She was not disorganized by nature. She was scared. Every time she tried to face her finances, it felt like stepping into a dark room with no flashlight. The questions were too big. What if she had made a catastrophic mistake? What if she owed more than she thought? What if the IRS was already looking at her?

Emma had grown her marketing agency from a dining-table side hustle to a multi six-figure operation in three years. On paper, she was thriving. Her *LinkedIn* told a story of upward momentum. Her client list was growing. Revenue had crossed the half-million mark.

But behind the scenes, her finances were held together with duct tape and denial.

She had four bank accounts across three banks, and she could not remember why she had opened half of them. Personal expenses and business expenses lived in the same account, like estranged roommates. She had subscriptions she did not remember signing up for, deducting quietly every month like tiny invisible leaks in a pipe she never checked.

Her bookkeeper sent her reports that she did not understand. Her accountant only called in March, and the conversation always felt like a scolding. When either of them asked a question about her numbers, Emma froze.

She did not have an answer. She only had a feeling. And the feeling was shame.

I know that feeling. Not because a client described it to me. Because I have lived my own version of it.

There was a season, years ago, when my husband and I bought a business we believed we could transform. We saw the financial challenges, but we convinced ourselves we could do it better than the previous owner. We chased the shiny object, believing it would accelerate our future. Instead, it drained much of the wealth we had worked so hard to build and placed more strain on our marriage than either of us expected. We came through it, but only because we finally stopped protecting each other from the numbers and started facing them together, at the same table, at the same time.

That experience changed me. It taught me that financial knowledge alone isn't enough. Even the smartest business owners can let optimism cloud judgment. Lasting wealth isn't built by chasing every opportunity. It's built by making intentional decisions, protecting what you've earned, and having the courage to walk away from opportunities that don't align with your long-term vision.

So when Emma sat on her bedroom floor that Tuesday night, surrounded by envelopes and shame, I did not judge her. I recognized her. She was me, years earlier, in a different room.

One afternoon, while Lily practiced pirouettes in the living room, Emma noticed a Post-it note stuck to the corner of her bathroom mirror. She did not remember having written it. In her own handwriting, it said:

If you want to grow, start by seeing where you are.

Something cracked open inside her. Not confidence. Not motivation. Something quieter. Permission.

She walked back to her bedroom, sat down on the floor again, and picked up the first envelope.

It was time.

The Strategy: Building Your Financial Fortress

Before we organize a single receipt or discuss a single write-off, we need to build something more important than a spreadsheet. We need to build safety.

Financial avoidance is not a numbers problem. It is a nervous system problem. When your relationship with money is rooted in fear, every interaction with your accounts triggers a fight-or-flight response. You do not need more discipline. You need a structure that makes it safe to look.

That is what this pillar is about. Fortifying your foundation means creating a financial environment where clarity is easy, confusion has nowhere to hide, and you can make confident decisions from a grounded place.

Here is how we do it.

Step One: Simplify Your Account Structure

Complexity is the enemy of clarity. If you have accounts scattered across multiple banks with no obvious purpose assigned to each one, your money has no home. Money without a home wanders. And wandering money creates anxiety.

Every woman entrepreneur needs three core business accounts, plus your fully separate personal account and retirement accounts, but we will get to that in the following chapters.

1) A Business Operating Account. This is where your revenue lands and your business expenses are paid. One account. One purpose. Everything that touches your business flows through here.

2) A Tax Reserve Account. This is a separate savings account where you move a set percentage of every deposit the moment it arrives. This is not optional. This is how you stop being ambushed by tax season. We will go deeper into this in Chapter 2, but the account needs to exist now.

3) A Savings Account. This is separate from the operating and completely separate from the Tax Reserve Account. This is where you'll really start to build your peace of mind and wealth. Just as you should have an emergency savings account personally, your business should have one with a goal of 3-6 months of savings.

That is it. Three accounts. Three purposes. If you have seven accounts and a drawer full of debit cards, it is time to consolidate. Simplicity is not basic. Simplicity is the most sophisticated foundation you can build.

Step Two: Create a Weekly Money Ritual

Avoidance thrives in the dark. The antidote is a short, consistent rhythm of visibility.

I want you to block twenty minutes every Friday. Not an hour. Not a full afternoon of anxiety. Twenty minutes. Pour yourself a cup of tea or coffee. Close the browser tabs. Put your phone in another room. This is not a time for multitasking. This is your appointment with your own financial truth.

During those twenty minutes, you do three things. First, you review what came in. Second, you review what went out. Third, you notice. That is it. You are not fixing anything in those twenty minutes. You are not reorganizing your entire chart of accounts or calling your accountant in a panic. You are just looking. You are training your nervous system to associate your finances with calm observation instead of crisis management.

Here is what most people do not understand about financial avoidance. It is not laziness. It is protection. Your brain learned at some point that looking at your money was dangerous, that the numbers would confirm something terrible about you. The weekly ritual retrains that response. It teaches your body that you can look and survive. That you can see a hard number and not spiral. That data is not a threat. It is a tool.

Over time, this ritual will become the most powerful habit in your financial life. It replaces dread with data. It replaces shame with sight. And it gives you something you have not had in a long time: a relationship with your money that feels safe.

Step Three:
Separate Business from Personal, Completely

Co-mingling personal and business expenses is the single most common structural mistake I see in the first year of working with any client. It is also the most damaging.

When business and personal expenses live in the same account, you cannot see your true profit. You cannot track your real expenses. And you are creating a compliance risk that could cost you dearly if the IRS ever looks closely.

The fix is not complicated. Stop using your business debit card for personal purchases. Stop transferring random amounts from your business account to cover household expenses. Set up a consistent pay schedule for yourself and honor it the same way you would honor payroll for an employee. Because that is exactly what it is.

Step Four: Know Your Baseline Numbers

You do not need to become an accountant. But you need to know numbers at all times. Your monthly revenue. Your monthly expenses. Your monthly profit. Your cash runway, which is how many months your business can survive if new revenue stopped today. And your gross profit margin percentage. This lets you know how profitable you are on your billing and helps you understand your true fixed costs.

These numbers are your financial vital signs. A doctor does not need to run a hundred tests to know if you are stable. She checks your heart rate, your blood pressure, your temperature, and your oxygen level. If those are steady, the rest can be explored calmly. If one of them is off, she knows exactly where to look.

Your business works the same way. When you know these five numbers without needing to scramble for them, you stop making decisions from fear and start making them from information. You can say yes to an investment because you know your runway supports it.

You can say no to a discount because you know your margins cannot absorb it. You can breathe.

If you cannot answer those five questions right now, without opening a single app, that is your sign. The foundation is not fortified yet. And that is okay. That is why you are here.

Your Foundation Fortress Checklist

Use this checklist to assess where you stand today. Every unchecked box is not a failure. It is your next step.

- I have a dedicated business checking account that is separate from my personal accounts.
- I have a separate tax reserve savings account, and I transfer a set percentage of revenue into it with every deposit.
- I have a structured pay schedule for myself, with consistent transfers from my business to my personal account.
- I have canceled or consolidated unnecessary accounts, cards, and subscriptions that create clutter.
- I have a weekly Money Ritual on my calendar (20 minutes, same day each week).
- I know my monthly revenue, expenses, profit, and cash runway without needing to look them up.
- My bookkeeping software is current and synced (QuickBooks, Xero, Wave, or equivalent).

- I have not used my business debit card for a personal purchase in the last 30 days.
- I have at least one month of operating expenses saved as a cash reserve.
- I feel safe, not scared, when I open my bank account.

Your Tool: The Monthly Money Clarity Map

The Monthly Money Clarity Map is a one-page snapshot of your financial truth. It is not a budget. Budgets tell you what you should do. This map tells you what is actually happening.

Each month, you will fill in five sections.

Section One: What Came In. Total revenue received this month, broken into categories if applicable (client payments, product sales, affiliate income, and so on).

Section Two: What Went Out. Total expenses, separated into fixed costs (rent, software, insurance) and variable costs (advertising, contractors, travel).

Section Three: What Stayed. Your profit for the month, which is simply what came in minus what went out. This number is not a judgment. It is a compass.

Section Four: What I Notice. This is the most important section. In two or three sentences, write what you observe. A subscription you forgot about. A client payment that came in late. A pattern you are starting to see. This section trains your financial awareness like a muscle.

Section Five: Gross Profit Margin. What is your percentage and what can be done to increase it? Remember, what gets reviewed changes.

Tape this map to the wall next to your desk, or keep it in a binder. At the end of each quarter, review all three maps side by side. You will start to see your money's story clearly, and you will make decisions from power instead of panic.

Scripts and Templates

Script 1: The Partner Money Meeting

If you share finances with a spouse or partner, this conversation is essential. Use the following language to open the dialogue without blame or defensiveness.

"I've been doing some work on our financial foundation, and I want to share what I'm learning. This is not about what we've done wrong. It's about what we can build together. Can we set aside thirty minutes this week to look at our numbers as a team? I want us both to feel confident and clear."

Script 2: The Bookkeeper Reset Conversation

If your bookkeeper sends reports you do not understand, the problem is communication, not intelligence. Use this language to reset the relationship.

"I want to get more involved in understanding my numbers. Going forward, can you send me a monthly summary that includes total revenue, total expenses, net profit, and my cash runway? I'd also love a five-minute walkthrough once a month so I can ask questions while it's fresh."

Script 3: The Self-Permission Statement

This one is for you. Say it out loud. Write it on a Post-it. Tape it to your mirror.

"I give myself permission to look at my money without shame.

What I see is just data. Data gives me the power to decide.

I am building something that will hold."

Emma's Shift

Within two weeks of opening that first envelope, Emma had consolidated her accounts down to three. She canceled four business subscriptions she had forgotten about — a duplicate project management platform, a premium CRM tier her team had stopped using, and two software tools that had been replaced months ago. The total savings: $873 per month.

She set up a weekly Friday Money Ritual with a cup of tea and twenty minutes of silence, and she started filling in her first Monthly Money Clarity Map.

The before and after was striking. Before the foundation work, Emma had four accounts with no assigned purpose, $2,100 per month in untracked subscriptions and duplicate tools, zero visibility into her profit margin, and a cash runway she could not calculate. After two weeks of fortifying, she had three accounts with clear roles, $873 in monthly savings from canceled waste, a profit margin she could name on the spot, and a cash runway of 2.4 months that she was now actively building toward four.

The first time she completed her Clarity Map, she cried. Not because the numbers were bad. Because she could finally see them.

She called me the following Monday. Her voice was steady in a way I had not heard before.

"I know my numbers, Sheena. For the first time, I actually know my numbers. I'm not guessing anymore. I'm not hiding. I feel like I just turned the lights on in a room I've been stumbling through for years."

Emma did not become a financial expert overnight. She did not overhaul her entire business in a weekend. She did something far more powerful than that. She built a foundation that could hold the weight of everything she was about to build next.

Her accounts had structure. Her schedule had a rhythm. Her nervous system had permission to exhale.

She was no longer guessing. She was grounded.

The Identity Shift

You did not pick up this book because you are bad with money. You picked it up because you are ready to build something stronger than what you have been standing on.

Fortifying your foundation is not glamorous work. It does not make for viral content or inspiring keynote moments. But it is the most important work you will do in this entire framework. Because every pillar that follows depends on this one. You cannot reduce your tax bill if you do not know your numbers. You cannot expand your wealth if your money has no structure. You cannot design a legacy on a foundation made of sand.

The woman who avoids her finances and the woman who leads them are not two different people. They are the same woman standing on two different foundations. One is built on fear. The other is built on clarity. You are crossing from one to the other right now, and that crossing does not require perfection. It requires honesty. It requires twenty minutes on a Friday. It requires three accounts with three purposes and the willingness to look at what is real.

This is where it starts. Not with a big win. With a quiet, courageous decision to look.

You have made that decision.

Your foundation is being fortified. And everything that comes next will be built on solid ground.

CHAPTER 2
Reduce Your Lifetime Tax Bill

F.R.E.E.D.O.M. Pillar Two

Stop overpaying the IRS and start directing your own money

There is a moment that most women entrepreneurs remember with perfect, painful clarity. It is the moment they open a tax bill and realize that the number staring back at them is larger than anything they spent on their family, their team, or themselves all year.

It arrives like a punch delivered in slow motion. You know it is coming somewhere in the back of your mind. But when the number appears on the screen or in the letter from your accountant, it still knocks the wind out of you.

You did everything you were told to do. You kept your receipts. You hired a bookkeeper. You filed on time. Even so, the government is taking a larger paycheck from your business than you are.

That is not a consequence of success. That is a symptom of a missing strategy.

And the worst part is not the money. The worst part is the feeling. The feeling that you are being punished for building something. The feeling that the harder you work, the more you hand over. The feeling that no matter how much you earn, you will never be allowed to keep enough of it to feel free.

That feeling is a lie. And this chapter is where we replace it with the truth.

The tax code is not your enemy. And the wealthy know this, it was designed for business owners and real estate investors. Why? Because the government rewards what it wants done. It wants the economy to grow with businesses, and it wants housing to be provided.

Here is the truth most women entrepreneurs are never told: the tax system does not reward hard work. It rewards planning. It rewards structure. It rewards the business owner who understands that taxes are not a fixed cost to be endured but a controllable expense to be managed.

You are not overpaying because you are irresponsible. You are overpaying because the system is built for those who plan ahead, and no one has taught you how to be one of them. Your accountant files your return. Your bookkeeper categorizes your transactions. But neither of them is building you a strategy. There is a difference between compliance and optimization, and that difference can be worth tens of thousands of dollars every single year.

Reducing your lifetime tax bill is not about loopholes. It is not about cheating. It is about learning the rules of a game that the wealthiest business owners have been playing for decades and finally giving yourself permission to play it, too.

Emma's Story:
The Forty-Two Thousand Dollar Wake-Up Call

Emma stood at the kitchen island, her laptop open, her accountant's voice coming through the phone on speaker. She was gripping the edge of the counter with both hands.

"As it stands, you're looking at about forty-two thousand."

Emma did not move. She stared at the number on the screen. Forty-two thousand dollars. She had worked sixty-hour weeks for twelve months. She had missed school plays, skipped vacations, turned down dinner invitations, and poured every ounce of herself into hitting her biggest revenue year yet. And now, in one sentence from a man she spoke to twice a year, nearly a quarter of her profit was evaporating.

"Forty-two thousand?" she repeated, her voice barely above a whisper.

The silence on the other end of the line said everything.

Emma had done what she thought was right. She had opened an LLC when a friend told her to. She had kept her receipts in a shoebox, then upgraded to a folder, then upgraded to a scanner app she used about half the time. She had hired a bookkeeper who sent monthly reports that she did not understand. She had an accountant who called in February, asked for documents she could never find fast enough, and delivered a number in April that always felt like a sentencing.

But no one had ever sat down with Emma and explained the difference between tax preparation and tax strategy. No one had told her that the structure of her business entity could change how every dollar she earned was taxed. No one had shown her that there were legal, ethical, and well-established methods to redirect thousands of dollars away from the IRS and back into her own life.

She had been playing a game she did not know existed. And she had been losing quietly for years.

That night, after her children were asleep, Emma sat in the dark of her living room and made a decision. Not a vague resolution. A decision with teeth.

"I will never feel powerless at tax season again."

She did not want to become a tax expert. She did not want to memorize the tax code. She wanted to understand enough to stop being a passenger in her own financial life. She wanted a strategy, not just a filing.

The next morning, she called my office.

The Plan: From Tax Compliance to Tax Strategy

When Emma and I sat down for our first strategy session, I asked her a question that changed the direction of her entire year.

"Emma, do you know the difference between what your accountant does and what a tax strategist does?"

She shook her head.

Most business owners do not know the difference, and it costs them dearly. A tax preparer records history. They look at what happened last year and report it to the IRS. That is important work, and it needs to be done correctly. But it is backward-looking by design. A tax strategist looks forward. They examine your current income, your business structure, your personal goals, and your growth trajectory, and they build a plan to legally minimize what you owe before the year is over.

The distinction between those two roles can be worth five figures or more every single year. And for most women entrepreneurs, no one has ever explained that the second one exists.

Here is what Emma learned, and what I want you to understand.

Strategy One: Your Entity Structure Matters More Than You Think

When Emma started her business, she filed as a sole proprietor because it was the simplest option. As her revenue grew, a friend told her to form an LLC, so she did. But no one explained what that LLC actually did for her tax bill. The answer, in her case, was nothing.

As a single-member LLC with no special election, Emma was still being taxed as a sole proprietor. Every dollar of profit was subject to self-employment tax on top of her regular income tax. That self-employment tax alone was costing her over fifteen percent on earnings that could have been structured differently.

We evaluated her revenue, her expenses, and her growth pattern, and we made the decision to elect S-Corporation status. This allowed Emma to pay herself a reasonable salary and take the remaining profit as a distribution, which is not subject to self-employment tax. The savings from that single structural shift were significant and immediate.

Entity structure is not a onetime decision you make when you launch your business and never revisit. It should be evaluated every year against your current income. What worked when you were earning sixty thousand may cost you when you are earning three hundred thousand. If your accountant has never raised this conversation with you, it is time to raise it yourself.

Strategy Two: Deductions Are Not Receipts in a Shoebox

Most business owners think of deductions as a collection of receipts. They save the coffee shop charges, the office supply runs, and the mileage logs, and they hope it adds up to something meaningful at tax time. That is the shallow end of the pool.

Real deduction strategy is about understanding the categories the tax code rewards and building your business operations to align with them. Home office deductions. Vehicle use. Professional development. Business travel. Retirement contributions through vehicles like a SEP IRA or Solo 401(k).

If you have employees on payroll, ask your strategist about a traditional 401(k) plan for your company. It is a bigger commitment, and it doubles as a benefit that helps you keep successful people. Health insurance premiums. Technology and equipment. Meals with clients where legitimate business is discussed and documented.

The keyword is documented. A deduction without documentation is a deduction that does not survive an audit. I tell every client the same thing: if you cannot prove it, you cannot claim it. That does not mean you need to be paranoid. It means you need a simple, consistent habit of recording the business purpose of every expense at the time it happens, not eight months later when your accountant asks.

Going Deeper: Three Strategies the Wealthy Use That Nobody Taught You.

Most deduction advice stops at the obvious: the home office, the mileage log, the software subscriptions. But there are three strategies that consistently surprise my clients, not because they are exotic, but because they are legal, well-established, and almost never explained to women entrepreneurs. Here they are.

Hiring Your Children

If your children do real, age-appropriate work in your business, such as filing, photography, modeling for your marketing, managing social media, or cleaning the office, you can pay them a reasonable wage for it. That wage is a deductible business expense. Because a child's standard deduction shields their first several thousand dollars of earned income, much or all of what you pay them can be entirely income-tax free to your child. You have just moved money from your highest tax bracket to their lowest one, and it never left the family. Even better, earned income makes your child eligible to fund a Roth IRA, which may be the single most powerful compounding gift you will ever give them. Two rules keep this clean: the work must be real and documented (timesheets, job descriptions, payment records), and the wage must be reasonable for the task. And one structural note: the payroll tax treatment differs depending on your entity type, so if you operate as an S-Corporation, talk with your strategist about how to structure this correctly before you run the first paycheck.

The Augusta Rule.

Buried in Section 280A(g) of the tax code is a provision that lets you rent out your personal home for up to fourteen days per year and pay zero income tax on that rental income. Here is where it becomes a strategy: your business can be the renter. Quarterly planning retreats, team trainings, client workshops, board meetings. If your business rents your home for a legitimate business purpose at a fair market rate, the business deducts the rent, and you receive the income tax-free. The documentation is what makes it survive scrutiny: a written rental agreement, evidence of the market rate for comparable meeting space in your area, a real agenda, and meeting minutes. Fourteen days. Fair market rate. Real business purpose. Paper trail. That is the whole recipe.

The Accountable Plan

If you have elected S-Corporation status, you may have noticed something frustrating: many of the deductions you took as a sole proprietor, like the home office, do not flow the same way anymore. The Accountable Plan is the fix. It is a written reimbursement arrangement under which your corporation reimburses you, the owner-employee, for business expenses you pay personally: a percentage of your home expenses for your office, your business mileage, and the business portion of your cell phone and internet. The corporation deducts every reimbursement. You receive the money completely tax-free. Without an Accountable Plan, those same dollars either go unclaimed or come to you as taxable wages. With one, they move from the business to your pocket without the IRS taking a bite. If you have an S-Corp and no Accountable Plan, this is a conversation to have with your strategist this month, not this year.

None of these strategies requires wealth to start. They require structure, documentation, and a strategist who brings them to you before December instead of after April. That is the difference between compliance and optimization, and it is measured in thousands of dollars, every single year.

Strategy Three: Tax Planning Is a Year-Round Practice

The most expensive mistake I see is treating taxes as an annual event. Tax season is not in April. Tax season is January through December.

When you wait until the end of the year to think about your tax bill, you have already missed the window for most meaningful strategies. Entity elections have deadlines. Retirement contributions have limits. Estimated quarterly payments need to be calculated and paid throughout the year, or you face penalties on top of your balance due.

Emma and I built what I call a Tax Flow Calendar. It is a simple quarterly rhythm. In the first month of each quarter, we reviewed her year-to-date income and projected her annual tax liability. We identified which strategies still had time to be implemented. We made adjustments. And we set aside the correct amount in her tax reserve account so that when April arrived, there were no surprises.

Proactive planning beats reactive scrambling every time. The goal is not to eliminate your tax bill. The goal is to make it predictable, manageable, and as low as the law allows.

Strategy Four: Build a Relationship With a Strategist, Not Just a Filer

Your CPA or accountant may be excellent at filing your return. But filing and strategizing are two different services, and not every professional offers both. If your tax professional only contacts you in the spring, only asks for documents, and never initiates a conversation about how to reduce your future liability, you do not have a strategist. You have a historian.

I encourage every woman reading this book to ask a direct question at your next meeting: "What can I do this year to legally reduce what I owe next year?" If the answer is vague, general, or amounts to "we'll see what happens," that is your signal. You deserve a partner who looks forward with you, not just backward for you.

Your Tax Reduction Checklist

Use this checklist to evaluate your current tax position. Every unchecked box is a conversation waiting to happen.

- I know my current business entity type (Sole Prop, LLC, S-Corp, C-Corp) and I understand why it was chosen.
- I have evaluated whether my entity structure still matches my current income level within the last twelve months.
- I have a dedicated tax reserve account, and I transfer a percentage of every deposit into it automatically.
- I pay quarterly estimated taxes on time to avoid penalties and surprises.
- I have a system for documenting the business purpose of every deductible expense at the time it occurs.
- I am maximizing my retirement contributions through a SEP IRA, Solo 401(k), or equivalent vehicle.
- I have claimed my home office deduction (if applicable) using the correct method for my situation.
- I track business mileage consistently using an app or log throughout the year.
- I meet with my tax professional at least quarterly, not just at filing time.

- I have asked my tax professional the question: "What can I do this year to reduce what I owe next year?"
- I have evaluated whether hiring my children in my business fits my situation.
- I have asked my strategist whether the Augusta Rule applies to me.
- If I have an S-Corporation, I have a written Accountable Plan in place.

Your Tools: The Business Expense Categorizer and Tax Vault Planner

This chapter comes with two tools that work together.

Tool One: The Business Expense Categorizer

This is a simple reference sheet that lists the most common deductible expense categories for women entrepreneurs, along with what qualifies under each one and what documentation is required to support the claim. Keep it next to your desk or save it on your phone. When you are unsure whether something is deductible, check the categorizer before you guess. Guessing is how money gets left on the table. It is also how expenses get claimed that should not be, which creates risk.

The categories include home office, vehicle and mileage, professional development and education, technology and software, marketing and advertising, travel and meals, insurance, retirement contributions, and professional services. Each category has a one-line description of what qualifies and a note on what records you need to keep.

Tool Two: The Tax Vault Planner

The Tax Vault Planner is a quarterly worksheet that helps you project your tax liability and track your reserve deposits. Each quarter, you fill in four numbers: your year-to-date revenue, your year-to-date deductible expenses, your projected annual income based on current pace, and the amount currently sitting in your tax reserve account.

The planner then walks you through a simple calculation to determine whether you are on track, ahead, or behind on your tax savings. If you are behind, it tells you exactly how much to deposit before the next quarter. If you are ahead, it gives you permission to breathe.

The goal of both tools is the same: to make taxes feel manageable instead of terrifying. When you can see what you owe, name what you can deduct, and track what you have saved, tax season stops being a crisis and starts being a checkpoint.

Scripts and Templates

Script 1: Questions to Ask Your CPA or Tax Professional

Bring this list to your next meeting. These are not aggressive questions. They are informed ones. A good tax professional will welcome them.

“Is my current entity structure optimized for my income level this year?”

“What deductions am I currently missing or underutilizing?”

“Should I be making quarterly estimated payments, and if so, how much?”

“What retirement account do you recommend for my situation?”

“What can I do between now and December 31st to reduce my tax liability for this year?”

“Are there any upcoming tax law changes I should prepare for?”

“Do any advanced strategies apply to my situation, such as hiring my children, the Augusta Rule, or an Accountable Plan? If so, what documentation would I need?”

Script 2: The Entity Structure Conversation Starter

If you have never discussed your entity structure in detail, use this language to open the conversation with your accountant or a new advisor.

"I want to make sure my business entity is still the best fit for where I am now. My revenue has changed since I first set this up, and I want to understand whether a different structure could reduce my self-employment tax or overall liability. Can we look at the numbers together and compare my options?"

Script 3: The Tax Season Affirmation

This one is yours. Say it before every quarterly review. Write it on the inside cover of this book.

"I am not afraid of my tax bill.

I plan for it. I prepare for it. I manage it with intention.

Every dollar I keep is a dollar I earned the right to direct."

Emma's Shift

Three months after our first strategy session, Emma called me. Her voice was shaking, but it was not the tremor of panic I had heard the first time we spoke. It was a relief.

"I just reviewed your projections, Sheena, we've saved over fifteen thousand dollars! I didn't land a new client.

I didn't launch anything new. I just changed the structure."

The before and after told the story clearly. Before the strategy work, Emma was operating as a single-member LLC taxed as a sole proprietor. She had no quarterly payment schedule, no tax reserve, and no proactive advisory relationship. Her previous year's tax bill was forty-two thousand dollars, and she had no idea it was coming until April.

After implementing just three changes, her projected tax bill for the current year dropped by over fifteen thousand dollars. She had elected S-Corporation status. She had set up a quarterly Tax Flow Calendar with reserve deposits automated. And she had documented deductions in real time instead of reconstructing them at year-end.

She did not work more hours. She did not earn a single extra dollar. She simply stopped leaving money on the table that was always hers to keep.

The Identity Shift

You were never meant to hand over a quarter of your effort to a system you do not understand. Taxes are a part of running a business, and paying them is a responsibility you should feel good about meeting. But overpaying is not a responsibility. Overpaying is the cost of not having a plan.

Dreading April is not a personality trait. It is a symptom of not having a plan. When you know your number months before the deadline, tax season stops being a verdict and becomes a line item. You stop waiting and hoping. You start planning and directing. You began that shift when you fortified your foundation. You are continuing it now by taking control of the single largest controllable expense in your business.

You are not cheating anyone by keeping more of your money. You are not gaming a system that was designed to be gamed. You are simply learning the rules and choosing to play with intention.

That is not avoidance. That is leadership.

Your tax bill will never surprise you again. And the money you keep will fuel everything that comes next.

Because keeping more cash is only the beginning. Now we make it grow.

CHAPTER 3
Expand Your Wealth

F.R.E.E.D.O.M. Pillar Three

Your business funds your freedom. Now make your money build a life beyond the hustle.

In Chapter 1, you built your three core business accounts. The wealth account is the fourth account in your system, and it is intentionally different: it is personal, it lives at a separate institution, and its job is not to run your business but to buy your freedom.

You can earn a great income and still be broke.

That sentence should not be true. But for millions of women entrepreneurs, it is the quiet, corrosive reality they live with every month. Revenue goes up. Lifestyle adjusts to match. A better office. A nicer car. A huge mortgage payment. And at the end of the year, after all the effort and all the growth, the savings account looks almost exactly the way it did twelve months ago.

You are not failing. You are caught in a cycle that no one warned you about. It is the cycle of earning and consuming without ever building. Income arrives, obligations absorb it, and the idea of wealth, of real wealth, of money that works while you sleep, stays pinned to a someday that never comes.

Most women were never taught the difference between income and wealth. Income is what you earn. Wealth is what stays. Income depends on your effort. Wealth depends on your system. And until you build that system, you will always feel like you are running on a treadmill that speeds up every time you take a step forward.

This chapter is about stepping off the treadmill. Not by earning less. Not by living smaller. By building a structure that takes the money you are already keeping and gives it a job that does not require your presence, your energy, or your time.

Wealth is not a salary. Wealth is a system.

You do not build wealth by working harder. You build it by creating a structure where your money multiplies without you. That means shifting your identity from earner to builder. From someone who trades time for dollars to someone who directs dollars into assets that generate returns on their own.

This is not about becoming a Wall Street trader or a real estate mogul overnight. It is about installing one simple belief into the operating system of your financial life: every dollar you keep should have a job. Some dollars pay for today. Some dollars protect against emergencies. And some dollars, the ones that will ultimately set you free, go to work building your future.

You have already fortified your foundation. You have already reclaimed cash through tax strategies. Now the question is no longer how to keep more. The question is what to do with what you have kept. This pillar is the answer.

Emma's Story:
The Day She Almost Bought the Trophy

Emma sat in my office three months after we restructured her taxes. For the first time in her entrepreneurial life, she had money that was not already spoken for. Her tax reserve was funded. Her operating account was stable. And there was a surplus sitting in her business savings that she had never seen before.

She leaned forward in her chair, her eyes bright with a mixture of excitement and guilt.

“I want to buy the Infiniti QX80,” she said. “I know that sounds ridiculous. But I’ve worked so hard, and I want to see the success when I walk out to my driveway. I want proof that all of this was worth it.”

I understood that impulse more than she knew. When you have spent years grinding, sacrificing, and questioning whether any of it will ever pay off, the first moment of breathing room creates an almost primal urge to reward yourself. You want the trophy. You want the tangible, visible evidence that you've made it. The car, the renovation, the vacation you could not afford to take last year.

There is nothing wrong with wanting those things. But I asked Emma a question that changed the way she thought about every dollar she would earn from that point forward.

"Do you want to look wealthy, or do you want to be wealthy? Because a car loses value the moment you drive it home. An asset gains value while you sleep."

Emma went quiet. Not because the question offended her. Because it landed somewhere deep.

She had never been taught to think about money in terms of what it could do for her beyond the immediate moment. Her parents had lived paycheck to paycheck. Her early career had been about survival. Even now, at the height of her earning power, her instinct was still to consume rather than build.

"So, what do I do with it instead?" she asked.

"We'll expand it," I told her. "We take the money you fought to keep, and we put it somewhere it can grow without needing you to show up every morning."

That conversation was the beginning of Emma's shift from business owner to wealth builder.

The Strategy: Building Your Wealth Expansion System

Expanding your wealth is not complicated. But it does require a shift in how you think about the money that flows through your life. Most entrepreneurs treat profit as leftovers. Whatever is still sitting in the account after expenses, taxes, and lifestyle gets labeled as savings, if it gets labeled at all. That is backward.

Wealth builders treat profit as a first allocation, not a last resort. As Mike Michalowicz teaches in Profit First, the discipline of paying yourself first changes everything. They move money into growth before lifestyle has a chance to absorb it. They automate the transfer, so willpower is never a factor. And they review their assets quarterly to ensure their money is working as hard as they are.

Here is the structure I teach.

Step One: Automate Your Wealth Allocation

The single most effective wealth-building habit you can install is automation. Human willpower is unreliable. Systems are not. The moment revenue hits your operating account, a percentage should move automatically into each account. This is based on the Profit First philosophy, but so much simpler!

1) Wealth Building

2) Emergency Fund

3) Taxes

4) Operating Expenses - leave this in your main account.

The percentage matters far less than consistency. But you need a starting point, so here is my recommendation. If you are under two hundred fifty thousand dollars in annual revenue, begin with fifteen percent to your tax reserve, ten percent to wealth building, and five percent to your emergency fund, with the rest staying in operations. If your margins are tight, cut every number in half and start anyway. A five percent transfer that happens every week will out build a twenty percent transfer that happens someday. You will refine these percentages with your strategist as your numbers become clear. The point is not precision on day one. The point is motion.

You are not trying to get rich in one transfer. You are installing a pattern that your money will follow for the rest of your life. Over time, you will increase the percentage. But the habit starts now.

The best way to start is by taking your total revenue and dividing it across each bucket account you set up in Chapter 1. Assign a percentage to your operating account, your tax reserve, your savings, and your wealth account. Even if the percentages feel imperfect at first, the act of splitting your money with intention changes your relationship to every dollar that moves through your business.

Step Two: Separate Wealth from Operating Cash

Your wealth account needs to live in a place where you cannot accidentally spend it. If it sits in the same bank as your business checking, the temptation to dip into it during a slow month will be real. I have watched too many clients build a beautiful savings balance only to drain it because the transfer was one click away. Proximity creates permission. Distance creates discipline.

Open a high-yield savings account or a brokerage account at a separate institution. Give it a name that means something to you. Some of my clients label theirs *Freedom Fund*. Others call it *Legacy*. One named hers *The Exhale*.

The label matters more than you might think. When your wealth account has a name and a purpose, it stops being an abstract pile of money and starts being a promise you are making to your future self. Money with a name does not wander. It works.

Step Three: Choose Your Growth

Once your wealth account has a consistent flow of deposits, you need to decide where that money will grow. There is no single correct answer. The right vehicle depends on your timeline, your risk tolerance, your income level, and your personal values. But here are the most common starting points for women entrepreneurs building their first layer of real wealth.

Retirement accounts. A SEP IRA or Solo 401(k) allows self-employed business owners to contribute significantly more than a traditional IRA. The tax benefits are immediate, and the compounding over time is powerful. If you are not maximizing your retirement contributions, this is often the first place to look.

Index funds in a brokerage account. For money you want to grow but access before retirement age, a taxable brokerage account with low-cost index funds offers simplicity and broad market exposure. You do not need to pick individual stocks. You need a strategy that grows steadily and does not require your daily attention.

Real estate. Whether it is a rental property, a real estate investment trust, or a small commercial space, real estate can provide both appreciation and ongoing income. It is not a starting point for everyone, but for entrepreneurs with stable cash flow and a longer timeline, it is one of the most reliable wealth-building vehicles in history.

Health Savings Accounts. If you have a qualifying high-deductible health plan, an HSA offers a triple tax advantage: contributions are tax-deductible, growth is tax-free, and withdrawals for qualified medical expenses are tax-free. Many entrepreneurs overlook this vehicle entirely. It is one of the most efficient tools available.

You do not need all of these at once. You need one. Choose the vehicle that aligns with where you are today and let the system do the work.

Step Four: Track Your Net Worth Monthly

Revenue is a measure of activity. Net worth is a measure of wealth. They are not the same thing, and the sooner you start tracking net worth, the sooner your financial decisions will shift from short-term to long-term thinking.

Net worth is simple. It is everything you own minus everything you owe. Add up your assets: cash, investments, retirement accounts, real estate, and the value of your business. Subtract your liabilities: loans, credit cards, and mortgages. The number that remains is your net worth. It is the truest measure of your financial life, because it cannot be inflated by a good revenue month or hidden by a busy one.

And here is a question worth asking: when was the last time your financial advisor built a real plan around your net worth and your goals, not just the products they manage? If the answer is never, it may be time for a new advisor.

I have watched clients go from avoiding their bank accounts entirely to opening their net worth tracker with the same calm they bring to checking the weather. That transformation does not happen because the numbers are always good. It happens because the act of looking consistently removes the power that financial uncertainty holds over your body and your decisions.

Set a recurring date each month to update your net worth. A simple spreadsheet or a free tracking app is more than enough. Watch the number over time. Watch it climb. Let that climb become the motivation that no trophy purchase could ever provide.

Your Wealth Expansion Checklist

Use this checklist to assess your current wealth-building position. Every unchecked box is your next priority.

- I have a dedicated wealth account that is separate from my business operating and tax reserve accounts.
- I have automated a monthly or per-deposit transfer into my wealth account.
- My wealth account has a meaningful name that connects it to my long-term purpose.
- I am contributing to a retirement vehicle (SEP IRA, Solo 401(k), Roth IRA, or equivalent).
- I know whether I am eligible for an HSA and whether I am utilizing it.
- I have chosen at least one growth path for my surplus cash (index fund, real estate, brokerage account).
- I track my net worth monthly using a spreadsheet or an app.
- I know the difference between my monthly revenue and my actual net worth.
- I have not dipped into my wealth account for lifestyle or operating expenses in the past 90 days.
- I can describe my wealth-building strategy in one sentence.

Your Tool: The Dream Funding Plan

The Dream Funding Plan is a one-page quarterly worksheet designed to connect your wealth-building actions to your actual financial goals. It is not a wish list. It is a document for your future.

The worksheet has three sections.

Section One: Define the Dream. What are you building toward? Be specific. Not *financial freedom,* but *the ability to take eight weeks off per year without a revenue drop*. Not *wealth,* but *a rental property generating three thousand dollars per month in passive income by 2030*. The clearer the target, the more powerful the plan.

Section Two: Fund the Dream. How much do you need to set aside each month to reach that target? Work backward from the goal. If your dream requires one hundred and fifty thousand dollars in five years, that is two thousand five hundred per month. If that number feels too large today, what is the starting amount you can automate this week, and how will you increase it over time?

Section Three: Protect the Dream. What boundaries do you need to set to prevent this money from being redirected? What triggers might tempt you to pull from this account, and what will you do instead? This section builds the guardrails that keep your dream funded even when life gets expensive.

Fill in your Dream Funding Plan at the start of each quarter. Review it alongside your Monthly Money Clarity Map and your Tax Vault Planner. Together, these three tools create a financial rhythm that is clear, grounded, and forward-moving.

Scripts and Templates

Script 1: Setting Up Your Automated Transfer

Call your bank or log into your online portal, or use your mobile app. Use this language to create your wealth automation.

"I want to set up a recurring automatic transfer from my [business checking/personal checking] account to my [wealth/investment] account. The amount is [dollar amount or percentage]. The frequency is [weekly/biweekly/monthly]. I want this to begin on [date]."

It should take less than ten minutes. It will change the trajectory of your financial life.

Script 2: Naming Your Wealth Accounts

Most banks allow you to rename your accounts in the app or online dashboard. Choose a name that makes you feel something when you see it. Here are examples from real clients.

Freedom Fund

Legacy Builder

The Exhale

Lily's Future (named for a child)

Red Hotel Fund (a personal wealth milestone)

CEO Wealth

The name should feel sacred to you. This is not a checking account you dip into for groceries. This is the container for the life you are building.

Script 3: The Wealth Identity Affirmation

Say this out loud. Tape it next to your Self-Permission Statement from Chapter 1.

"I am no longer just an earner. I am a builder.

My money has a job beyond today.

Every dollar I direct toward my future is proof that I trust myself with wealth."

Emma's Shift

Emma did not buy the Infiniti QX80.

Instead, she opened a high-yield savings account and a brokerage account at a separate bank, and she named the savings account The Red Hotel. She automated a transfer of fifteen percent of her monthly revenue into it. Within two months, it held more than she had ever saved in her life.

She opened a 401(k), something she could have done even back when she was a sole proprietor, though no one had ever told her. She funded it, contributing the maximum her new salary allowed, and for the first time, her team had a retirement benefit too. The brokerage account had a simple index fund allocation and was set to receive five hundred dollars per month on autopilot.

The before and after told a story that numbers alone could not fully capture. Before the expansion work, Emma had zero invested outside of an old employer 401(k) that she had not checked in years. Her savings balance fluctuated with every slow month. She had no net worth tracking system and no growth path in place. After three months of expansion, she had a funded 401k, an active brokerage account, a wealth reserve with a five-figure balance, and a net worth she updated on the first of every month.

But the real shift was not in the numbers. It was in her posture. She sat differently in meetings. She made decisions differently. She stopped chasing every new client as if her survival depended on it, because for the first time, her survival did not depend on next month's revenue alone.

"I used to think wealth was for other people," she told me. "People with trust funds or stock portfolios handed to them. I never thought I could build it from scratch. But here I am, building it. And it's working."

The Identity Shift

There is a line that most women entrepreneurs never cross. On one side is the earner. She works hard, makes good money, and spends it well. On the other side is the builder. She works hard, makes good money, and directs a portion of it into structures that will outlast her effort.

Crossing that line does not require a finance degree. It does not require a windfall or an inheritance. It requires one automated transfer, one growth path, and one decision to stop treating wealth as something that happens to other people.

You have fortified your foundation. You have reduced your tax bill. And now you have begun directing the money you fought to keep toward a future that does not depend on your constant presence. That is expansion. That is the third pillar. And it changes everything that follows.

Nobody becomes a builder by accident. It happens the day one automated transfer leaves your account and you do not move it back. You now have the system. And every month that it runs, the gap between where you were and where you are going grows wider in your favor.

Your wealth is expanding. And it will keep expanding long after you close this book.

Because wealth without joy is just another kind of prison.

YOUR FREE CALCULATOR SUITE

Access your S Corp Tax Savings Calculator, Freedom Number

Calculator and Tax Reserve Calculator.

YOUR FREE CALCULATOR SUITE

Access your S Corp Tax Savings Calculator, Freedom Number Calculator and Tax Reserve Calculator.

shebuildswealthy.com/calculators

CHAPTER 4
Elevate Your Lifestyle

F.R.E.E.D.O.M. Pillar Four

Build a business that funds the life you want to live.

You have done the hard part.

You fortified your foundation. You restructured your taxes. You started building wealth. Chapter 3 was about making smarter choices with your money. This chapter is about creating a business that funds the life you deserve. Not someday. Now.

There is a pattern in entrepreneurship that no one talks about honestly. It is the pattern of hustle culture dressed up as discipline. Work more. Sacrifice more. Defer every pleasure until later, and later never arrives. You are told that grinding is the price of success, that rest is for people who have not earned it yet, and that every dollar spent on yourself is a dollar stolen from your business. That is not a strategy. That is a trap. And this chapter is where you walk out of it.

You have spent your entire financial life earning the right to enjoy what you build. But no one ever told you that the right was already yours.

This chapter is not about spending more. It is about spending with alignment. It is about giving yourself permission to experience the life your money was always meant to fund.

Here is the truth hustle culture will never tell you: you can defer every glee, delay every reward, and postpone your entire life until some finish line that keeps moving, and the finish line will never arrive.

That is not discipline. That is deprivation wearing a suit.

True financial health includes enjoyment. It includes rest. It includes the ability to look at your bank account and say, with full confidence, "I have taken care of my future, and I am allowed to enjoy my present." That is not reckless. That is the entire point.

Elevating your lifestyle does not mean inflating your spending. It means aligning your spending with what actually matters to you. It means stripping away the noise of guilt purchases, stress spending, and obligations that drain your account without feeding your soul, and replacing them with intentional investments in the experiences, comforts, and rituals that make your life feel like yours.

You do not need to earn more to feel rich. You need to spend with intention. And you need to stop apologizing for the parts of your life that bring you joy.

Emma's Story: The CEO Mastermind That Changed Everything

Emma called me on a Tuesday morning from a balcony in Scottsdale.

She had booked a four-day CEO mastermind in the desert. Not a trade conference. Not a networking happy hour. A small, curated room of twelve women business owners, facilitated by a coach Emma had followed for years. The agenda was not tactics or funnels. It was vision, leadership, and building a business that works for you instead of the other way around.

It was the first investment Emma had made in herself as a CEO, not as a service provider, in three years.

"I'm sitting here with coffee and a journal," she said, her voice lighter than I had ever heard it. "And for the first hour, I kept expecting a client emergency. I kept waiting for permission to be here. Like I had to justify the expense with an immediate ROI."

I let her sit with that for a moment. Then I said the thing she needed to hear.

"Emma, you are not stealing from your business. You are investing in the only person who can lead it. A CEO who never steps back to think is not leading. She is surviving."

The silence on her end was not uncomfortable. It was the silence of something landing. Something shifting.

Emma had spent years pouring herself into everyone and everything else. Her clients got the best of her energy. Her children got whatever was left. Her husband got the tired version. And she got nothing. Not because she could not afford it, but because hustle culture had convinced her that investing in herself was selfish.

That belief did not come from nowhere. It came from watching her mother work double shifts without ever taking a day for herself. It came from a culture that celebrates the woman who grinds and side-eyes the one who rests. It came from a business world that measures your worth by how many hours you log, not by how clearly you think.

That voice is not wisdom. That voice is hustle culture dressed up as discipline. And this is where you turn the volume down.

By the third day of the mastermind, something had shifted. Emma was not checking her phone under the table. She was not calculating the cost per hour. She was sitting in a room full of women who understood her, mapping out a twelve-month vision for her business, and thinking more clearly than she had in years.

She sent me a voice note that evening. "Sheena, I just realized something. Every system we have built, the foundation, the tax plan, the wealth account, they gave me the infrastructure to be here. I could not have invested in this mastermind a year ago. I would not have had the money or the confidence. The framework made this possible. And being here is honing me a CEO."

When I listened to that voice note, I had to set my phone down for a moment. Not because I was surprised by her breakthrough. Because it took me back to my own.

The first time I invested in myself after we lost nearly everything, I flew to Austin, Texas, for a high-level women's mastermind retreat. Walking into that room took everything I had. Every woman there was wildly successful, and I was the one rebuilding from a betrayal that had emptied our accounts and shaken my faith in my judgment.

During one session, the presenter asked us to score ourselves on where our businesses stood. I scored myself, which that year meant I scored myself low. A woman at my table looked at my number and said, loudly enough for the entire table to hear, that I was bringing down the table average.

I fought back tears in that seat. I will not pretend otherwise. But underneath the sting, something steadier rose, something that comment could not touch. I had built real success before. I knew exactly what it took to win because I had done it. The career, the investments, the businesses. My low score was not my ceiling. It was my starting line. And I was in that room on purpose, because rebuilding bigger requires rooms that stretch you, even when they sting.

Her comment did not send me home. It confirmed I was exactly where I needed to be.

That is what I heard in Emma's voice note from Scottsdale. The sound of a woman claiming her seat in the room and finally learning to receive what the room had to give her.

The Strategy: Spending With Alignment

Elevating your lifestyle is not about inflating your expenses. It is about auditing them for alignment. Most women entrepreneurs are spending plenty of money. The problem is that a surprising amount of that spending is driven by stress, guilt, obligation, or comparison rather than by genuine values.

Here is how to build a lifestyle that reflects who you actually are.

Step One: Conduct a Values-to-Spending Audit

Write down your top five values. Not the ones that sound impressive. The ones that are actually true. Family time. Health. Travel. Creativity. Simplicity. Spiritual growth. Learning. Connection. Whatever is real for you.

Then open your bank statement from the last thirty days and compare. How much of your spending went toward things that align with those values? And how much went toward things that do not serve you at all?

Most clients who complete this exercise discover a significant gap. They find recurring charges for services they never use, takeout orders driven by exhaustion rather than enjoyment, subscriptions they signed up for in a moment of aspiration and have not touched since. They find spending that is not bad, but is not aligned. And the gap between those two things is where your lifestyle elevation lives.

Step Two: Build a Joy Budget

I want you to create a line item in your personal budget that is labeled something you feel proud of. Call it *Lifestyle Elevation.* Call it *Joy.* Call it *The Permission Fund.* Whatever name makes you feel expansive instead of guilty.

This is not a slush fund. It is a structured, intentional allocation, typically five to ten percent of your take-home pay, that is designated for things that bring you genuine pleasure. Fresh flowers every week. A quarterly weekend getaway. A membership to a class that lights you up. A monthly dinner at a restaurant that makes you feel alive.

The act of budgeting for joy does something powerful to your nervous system. It removes the guilt. When the money is already allocated, already set aside, already approved by your own financial plan, spending it stops feeling like a transgression and starts feeling like a celebration. You are not splurging. You are honoring a line item that you created on purpose.

Step Three: Eliminate Noise Spending

Noise spending is any recurring expense that does not align with your values, does not bring you joy, and exists only because you have not paused long enough to question it. It is the streaming service you do not watch. The gym membership that you have not used in four months. The subscription box that felt exciting the first time and now sits unopened by the door.

Noise spending is different from waste. Waste implies carelessness. Noise implies distraction. You are not careless with your money. You are busy. And busy women accumulate financial noise without realizing it. It builds slowly, ten dollars here, thirty dollars there, until you have a few hundred dollars per month leaving your account for things that do not improve your life in any measurable way.

Go through your last three months of bank statements and highlight every recurring charge. For each one, ask a single question: does this actively serve my life or my values? If the answer is no, cancel it. Redirect that money toward your Joy Budget or your Wealth Account from Chapter 3. Every dollar you recover from noise spending is a dollar that can now fund something that matters.

Step Four: Practice Receiving Without Deflecting

This one is harder than it sounds. Many women have been trained to deflect abundance. Someone compliments your outfit, and you say, "Oh, this old thing." Someone asks how business is going, and you downplay your success to make them comfortable. Someone offers to buy you dinner, and you insist on splitting the check because receiving feels dangerous.

Receiving is a skill. And it is a skill that directly impacts your financial life. The woman who cannot receive a compliment without deflecting is often the same woman who cannot receive a profit without immediately giving it away, reinvesting it, or feeling guilty about it.

Start small. The next time someone compliments you, say, "Thank you." Full stop. No qualifier. The next time you have a profitable month, do not immediately reinvest every cent. Take a portion and spend it on something that makes you feel alive. Practice the act of receiving. Let abundance feel safe in your body. That safety is the foundation of a lifestyle that matches your success.

Your Lifestyle Alignment Checklist

Use this checklist to assess whether your lifestyle reflects your values. Every unchecked box is a chance to realign.

- I have identified my top five personal values and written them down.

- I have compared my spending over the last 30 days against those values and noted the gaps.
- I have created a Joy Budget line item with a specific monthly allocation.
- I have canceled at least one recurring subscription or expense that does not serve my values.
- I have redirected recovered funds toward my Joy Budget or Wealth Account.
- I have scheduled at least one experience this month that exists purely for my enjoyment.
- I can receive a compliment without deflecting or minimizing it .
- I can spend money on myself without guilt lasting longer than the moment of purchase.
- My calendar includes at least one non-negotiable appointment for rest, play, or personal enrichment each week.
- I believe, in my body and not just my mind, that I am allowed to enjoy the wealth I am building.

Your Tool: The CEO Pay Calculator and Joy Budget

This worksheet has two sides, and they are designed to work together.

Side One: The CEO Pay Calculator

Most women entrepreneurs do not pay themselves consistently. They take draws when the business account looks healthy and skip their pay when things feel tight. This creates a boom-and-bust relationship with personal income that keeps your nervous system in survival mode even when your business is thriving.

The CEO Pay Calculator walks you through four inputs: your average monthly revenue, your average monthly business expenses, your tax reserve percentage from Chapter 2, and your wealth transfer amount from Chapter 3. What remains after those allocations is your available owner pay. The worksheet then helps you set a consistent bi-weekly or monthly paycheck amount that you commit to for the next quarter.

Consistency is the point. When you know what you are paying yourself, and you know it is coming on the same day every period, you can plan your personal life with confidence instead of anxiety.

Side Two: The Joy Budget

Once you know your CEO pay number, you allocate a percentage to your Joy Budget. The worksheet prompts you to list three to five categories of joy spending that align with your values. It might include travel, dining, wellness, education, or creative hobbies. Each category gets a monthly allocation. The total becomes your guilt-free lifestyle fund.

At the end of each month, you review what you spent in each category. Not to judge yourself, but to notice. Are you using the fund? Are you still deflecting? Are there categories you are over-spending in versus others you are ignoring? The Joy Budget is not a restriction. It is a mirror. It shows you whether your money and your values are finally in the same room.

Scripts and Templates

Script 1: The Pay-Yourself Commitment

Use this language with yourself, your bookkeeper, or your accountant to formalize your CEO pay.

"Starting this month, I am setting a consistent owner's pay of [amount] on the [1st and 15th/last day] of every month. This is non-negotiable. Please set up the recurring transfer and treat it as payroll. I am paying myself the way I would pay any valued employee, because that is what I am."

Script 2: The Joy Budget Check-In

At the end of each month, ask yourself these three questions. Write the answers in your journal or on the back of your Joy Budget worksheet.

"What did I spend on joy this month that made me feel genuinely alive?

Where did I hold back from spending on myself, and what was the voice in my head telling me?

What would I like to experience next month that I have been putting off?"

Script 3: The Lifestyle Elevation Affirmation

This is yours. Say it before you open your Joy Budget each month. Let it dissolve the guilt before it has a chance to form.

"I have earned the right to enjoy my life.

My wealth is not just for the future. It is for right now.

I receive abundance with open hands and a clear conscience."

Emma's Shift

When Emma returned from the mastermind, she did not go back to the way things were. She sat down with her CEO Pay Calculator and set a consistent bi-weekly paycheck for the first time in her business. She created a Joy Budget that allocated eight percent of her take-home pay to experiences that aligned with her values: family adventures, solo retreats, weekly fresh flowers on her desk, and a monthly dinner date with her husband that was not interrupted by her phone.

The before and after was less about numbers and more about presence. Before the lifestyle work, Emma had no consistent pay schedule. She took draws when the account looked healthy and skipped herself when it did not. She spent reactively, often driven by stress: late-night online shopping, overpriced takeout on exhausting days, impulse purchases that sat unused. She could not remember the last time she spent money on herself and felt only joy.

After implementing the system, her personal income became predictable. Her Joy Budget was funded and used. On the personal side, she had canceled over six hundred dollars per month in noise spending—separate from the business waste she cut in Chapter 1—and redirected it toward things that mattered. She booked a quarterly solo retreat on her calendar for the rest of the year. And for the first time, she stopped downplaying her success at dinner parties.

She sent me a text three weeks later.

"Someone asked me how business was going, and I said, 'It's going beautifully.' I didn't qualify it. I didn't shrink. I just let the truth sit there. Sheena, that might be the biggest shift yet."

The Identity Shift

The woman who builds wealth but never enjoys it and the woman who enjoys her life while building wealth are not separated by income. They are separated by permission.

You have spent your entire career proving that you are responsible, disciplined, and worthy of the success you have created. You do not need to prove it anymore. The foundation is fortified. The taxes are managed. The wealth is growing. The structure is in place.

Now it is time to let your life catch up with your numbers.

Elevating your lifestyle is not the opposite of building wealth. It is the completion of it. Wealth that exists only on a spreadsheet and never touches your lived experience is incomplete wealth. The whole point of keeping more cash is to have more of your life available to you. More time. More peace. More experiences that fill you up instead of draining you dry.

You are allowed to enjoy this. You are allowed to receive this. And you do not need to shrink to make anyone else comfortable with your expansion.

Your lifestyle is elevating. And the woman who walks into the next chapter is no longer just a builder. She is a woman who is finally living the life her money was designed to support.

Because the most powerful thing you can build is something that outlives you.

CHAPTER 5
Design Your Legacy

F.R.E.E.D.O.M. Pillar Five

Wealth without intention dies with you. Legacy is built while you are alive.

Nobody wants to talk about this chapter.

Not because the content is complicated. Not because the strategies are hard. But because legacy planning forces you to sit with a question that most of us would rather avoid: what happens to everything I have built if I am suddenly not here to protect it?

That question touches something deeper than money. It touches mortality. It touches the quiet fear that the people you love most might be left in confusion, in conflict, or in a courtroom because you never wrote down what you wanted. It touches the guilt of knowing that you have poured years of effort into building something beautiful, and you have not yet taken the steps to ensure it survives you.

Most women put this off. They tell themselves they are too young. Too busy. Too early in the process. They say, "I'll handle it when things settle down," and things never settle down. Meanwhile, the business grows, the assets compound, and the gap between what they have built and what is legally protected gets wider every month.

This chapter is not morbid. It is the most loving thing you will ever do for the people who depend on you. It is not about the end of your story. It is about making sure your story continues exactly the way you intended.

Here is what nobody says out loud: legacy is not something you leave behind when you die. Legacy is something you design while you are alive.

It is the clarity you create so your family never has to guess what you wanted. It is the infrastructure you build so that your wealth does not evaporate in probate court. It is the values you articulate so that your children inherit not just your money, but your wisdom. It is the intention you pour into your business so it can outlive your daily presence.

Most women entrepreneurs have spent years building a financial life with structure, strategy, and heart. But without legacy planning, all that work is vulnerable. A business without a succession plan dissolves. Assets without a trust can be frozen for months or years. Children without clear guardianship designations become the subject of courtroom decisions made by strangers.

You did not build this far to leave the ending to chance. Legacy is not reserved for the ultra-wealthy. It is for anyone who has built something worth protecting. And if you are reading this book, you have.

Emma's Story: The Funeral That Changed Everything

The funeral was simple. A small chapel. White flowers. A folded program with a photo of a woman who looked like she could still walk through the door at any moment.

Emma sat in the third row, clutching the program in both hands. Her grandmother had been a quiet force in the family. Not loud about her money, not flashy about her success. She had run a small business for thirty years, raised four children, and held the family together through seasons that would have broken most people.

But what struck Emma that day was not the grief. It was what happened after the service.

The family gathered at Emma's aunt's house, and within an hour, the arguments started. Her grandmother had no will. No trust. No written instructions. There was a house, a savings account, and a business that no one knew how to run. Two of Emma's uncles had different memories of what their mother *wanted*. One aunt refused to speak to the other. The business, the one her grandmother had poured three decades into, closed within six months because there was no plan to keep it running.

Emma watched a lifetime of work dissolve into confusion, silence, and resentment. Not because her grandmother did not care. But because no one had ever told her that caring was not enough. You have to document it. You have to structure it. You have to say it out loud and put it in writing.

Three weeks after the funeral, Emma sat in my office with a look I had not seen on her face before. It was not panic. It was not sadness. It was resolve.

"I don't want that to be my story," she said. "I don't want Lily and Caleb fighting over something I could have made clear. I don't want my business to close because no one knew what to do. Sheena, I need a plan. A real one."

I nodded. "Then let's build one. Not because something is going to happen to you. But because you love the people in your life enough to give them clarity instead of chaos."

Emma leaned back in her chair and exhaled. "I thought legacy was about being rich enough to leave something behind. I'm starting to think it's about being brave enough to have the conversation."

She was right.

Emma was right. And I will tell you something now that costs me to admit. As I write this chapter, I still have not finished the crossing. My own legacy plan is not done. The woman who organizes everyone else's financial life has unfinished pages in her own. The crossing requires something expertise cannot supply. It requires an honest afternoon that no one can delegate, not even me.

I am not writing this chapter from the far shore, looking back at you. I am making the crossing with you. Every step I lay out below is the same list sitting on my desk. If you have been telling yourself you are too young, too busy, or too early, know that the woman writing this book told herself the same things for years. We are done with that story, you and I. Let this be the chapter we both finish.

Because a legacy plan is not paperwork. It is a love letter with a notary stamp.

When Emma sat across from me and said she wanted a plan, a real one, I did not hand her advice from a textbook. I gave it to her as a woman who knew exactly how long a person can know better and still not act, and who had decided that love without documentation is hope without a net.

The Strategy: Building Your Legacy

Legacy planning is not a single document. It has legal components, financial components, and emotional components. And every one of them matters.

Step One: Get Your Legal Foundation in Place

I am not a lawyer, and nothing in this chapter is legal advice. But there are five pillars of legacy protection that every woman entrepreneur should have in place, regardless of income level, age, or family situation. Four of them are legal documents. One of them is a financial safety net. All five are non-negotiable. Consult an estate attorney who understands your specific situation.

A Will. This is the most basic legal expression of your wishes. It states who receives your assets, who becomes guardian of your minor children, and who you trust to manage the process. Without a will, your state decides all of those things for you. That is not a risk worth taking.

Life Insurance. This is the pillar with the simplest job: if something happens to you, your family is protected. When most people think of life insurance, they think of an expense. A monthly premium you pay, hoping no one ever needs it. I think of it differently. It is the answer to a question every breadwinner must be able to face. If my income disappeared tomorrow, could my family keep their home, keep the business running, and keep the future we planned?

For most women entrepreneurs, the answer is a term policy. Affordable, straightforward, and large enough to replace your income and retire your debts. Pure protection, which is what your family needs most. More advanced insurance strategies exist for certain top earners, and if one is ever proposed to you, evaluate it the way you would evaluate any investment, with a fee-only advisor who does not earn a commission on your yes. But do not let the advanced conversation delay the essential one. Protection first. Everything else is optional.

A Living Trust. A trust allows your assets to bypass probate, which is the court-supervised process of distributing a deceased person's estate. Probate can be slow, expensive, and public. A properly funded trust keeps your affairs private, your family out of court, and your instructions intact. For business owners with real estate, investment accounts, or significant assets, a trust is not optional. It is essential.

A Power of Attorney. This document designates someone you trust to make financial decisions on your behalf if you become incapacitated. Without it, your family may need a court order to access your own accounts. That delay can be devastating during a medical emergency.

A Healthcare Directive. This document communicates your medical wishes if you are unable to speak for yourself. It names the person authorized to make healthcare decisions on your behalf and specifies the kind of care you want or do not want. This is not just a legal formality. It is an act of compassion for the people who love you.

These five pillars are the structural walls of your legacy. Without them, everything you have built sits exposed.

Step Two: Create a Succession Blueprint for Your Business

Your business is likely one of your most valuable assets. But unlike a bank account or a piece of real estate, a business does not transfer automatically. If you are the primary operator, the primary salesperson, and the primary relationship holder, your business has a vulnerability: you.

A succession blueprint answers three questions. First, who can run this business if you are unable to? This might be a team member, a partner, or a trained successor. Second, is the business structured to be sold, transferred, or wound down in an orderly way? Third, does anyone other than you know how the business actually works? If the answer to that last question is no, your business is not yet an asset. It is a dependency.

You do not need to have a full exit plan today. But you do need to begin documenting your processes, identifying your key people, and building a business that can function without your daily presence. This connects directly to Chapter 6, where we will optimize your operations. Legacy and operations are partners. *One without the other is incomplete.*

These steps allow you to build a business that leaves a value to your family. Unlike Emma's grandmother, your business will leave your children so much more without confusion and fighting.

Step Three: Write Your Legacy Letter

This is the document that no attorney can draft for you. It is the most personal piece of your legacy architecture, and in many ways, it is the most powerful.

A legacy letter is not a legal document. It is a letter from you to the people you love. It contains the things you want them to know. Your values. Your hopes for them. The lessons you learned the hard way that you wish someone had told you sooner. The reasons behind your financial decisions. The love you carry for them that may not always find its way into words during the rush of daily life.

Some of my clients write their legacy letters to their children. Others write them to their spouses, their business partners, or their communities. One client wrote hers to her younger self, and then shared it with her daughter as a way of saying, "This is where I came from. This is what I learned. And this is what I want for you."

There is no template for this letter. There is only honesty. Write it by hand if that feels right. Type it and print it if that feels more natural. Put it in a sealed envelope. Place it in a folder with your legal documents.

And update it every year, because you are not the same woman in December that you were in January. Your legacy letter should grow as you do.

Step Four: Have the Conversations

Documents without dialogue are incomplete. The people in your life need to know that a plan exists. They need to know where to find it. They need to know who your attorney is, where your trust documents are stored, and what your wishes are before they are standing in a chapel trying to remember.

This does not need to be a heavy, somber conversation. It can be simple. It can be brief. It can happen over dinner or during a walk. The point is not to deliver a speech. The point is to open a door. Once the door is open, the conversations become easier every time.

Your Legacy Design Checklist

Use this checklist to assess where your legacy architecture stands today. Every unchecked box is a conversation or an appointment waiting to happen.

- I have a current, signed will that reflects my wishes.
- I have established a living trust and funded it with my major assets.
- I have a designated power of attorney for financial decisions.

- I have a healthcare directive that names my medical decision-maker and outlines my care preferences.
- I have named and updated beneficiaries on all financial accounts, insurance policies, and retirement vehicles.
- I have identified at least one person who could operate or transition my business if I were unable to.
- I have documented my core business processes so they are not dependent on my personal knowledge alone.
- I have written a legacy letter to my loved ones and placed it with my legal documents.
- I have told at least one trusted person where my important documents are stored.
- I have scheduled an annual review of my legacy plan to keep it current as my life and assets evolve.

Your Tool:
The Love Letter and Legacy Prep Sheet

This worksheet is designed in two parts.

Part One: The Legacy Prep Sheet

This one-page document serves as a central inventory of your most important financial and estate planning information. It includes the location of your will and trust documents, along with the names and contact information for your estate attorney, financial advisor, and CPA. You'll also record your major assets, including account numbers and financial institutions, as well as your designated beneficiaries, power of attorney, healthcare proxy, and guardians for your children. In addition, there's a dedicated section to document your life insurance policies, making it easier for your loved ones to access the information they need when it matters most.

Think of this as the instruction manual for your financial life. If something happened to you tomorrow, could the person you trust most walk into your office and find everything they need? This sheet ensures the answer is yes. Fill it out, print two copies, and store one in a fireproof safe or safe deposit box and the other with your attorney or a trusted family member.

Part Two: The Love Letter

The second page is blank. It has only a single prompt at the top:

"To the people I love most: here is what I want you to know."

There are no rules. No formatting requirements. No character limits. Write what matters. Write what you have been meaning to say. Write the lessons you want your children to carry. Write the gratitude you feel for your partner. Write the vision you hold for the family you have built.

This letter is not a goodbye. It is a gift. And it is one of the most important pages you will ever write.

Scripts and Templates

Script 1: Opening the Legacy Conversation with Your Partner

If you have been avoiding this conversation, use this language to start. It is not heavy. It is honest.

"I've been thinking about something important, and I want to talk it through with you. I'm not worried about anything specific, but I want to make sure that if anything ever happened to either of us, the other person would not have to guess. I'd love for us to sit down this weekend and go through our plan together. It's one of the most loving things we can do for each other."

Script 2: Questions to Ask an Estate Attorney

Bring this list to your first consultation. An estate attorney will respect your preparation.

"Do I need a will, a trust, or both based on my current assets and family situation?"

"How do I properly fund a trust so my assets are protected?"

"What happens to my business entity if something happens to me?"

"Who should I name as guardian for my minor children, and what does that process look like?"

"How often should I update these documents, and what triggers a revision?"

"What is the difference between probate and non-probate assets, and are mine structured correctly?"

Script 3: The Legacy Affirmation

Say this before you write your love letter. Let it ground you in purpose, not fear.

"I am not planning for the end. I am designing for continuation.

My wealth deserves intention. My family deserves clarity.

The most powerful thing I can leave behind is a plan built with love."

Emma's Shift

Emma scheduled a meeting with an estate attorney the week after we talked. She brought her Legacy Prep Sheet, already half completed. She asked every question on the list and a few of her own. Within thirty days, she had a signed will, a living trust funded with her business ownership and real estate, a power of attorney, and a healthcare directive. And she set up life insurance.

The before and after was not measured in dollars. It was measured in peace. Before the legacy work, Emma had no will, no trust, no written instructions of any kind. Her business had no succession plan. Her children's guardianship was not formally designated. Her husband did not know the passwords to her financial accounts. If something had happened to her, her family would have faced months of legal uncertainty at the worst possible moment.

After thirty days, every major asset was titled in the trust. Her children's guardians were named. Her husband had access to the Legacy Prep Sheet and knew where every document was stored. And tucked inside the folder, in a sealed envelope, was her love letter.

She told me about writing it the following week. Her voice was quiet, but not sad.

"I sat down to write it thinking I'd knock it out in ten minutes. I ended up writing for two hours. I wrote to Lily and Caleb about who I hope they become. I wrote to my husband about why I chose him. And I wrote to myself about the woman I'm becoming. Sheena, it was the most clarifying thing I've ever done. Not because about dying. Because I'm finally clear about what I'm living for."

The Identity Shift

Legacy is not something the wealthy do after they retire. It is something the intentional do while they are building.

You have spent four chapters fortifying, reducing, expanding, and elevating. Every one of those pillars created something worth protecting. This chapter is where you protect it. Not with fear. With love. With the same clear-headed strategy you have applied to your taxes, your wealth, and your lifestyle.

Legacy planning does not require age, net worth, or readiness. It requires one honest afternoon with an attorney and one evening alone with a blank page. You have now had both.

Your legacy is no longer theoretical. It is documented. It is structured. And it carries your voice, your values, and your love into a future you may or may not be present for.

That is not morbid. That is the bravest kind of motherhood, partnership, and leadership there is.

You have designed your legacy. Now it is time to build the systems that support it.

Because an empire cannot run on one woman's shoulders forever.

CHAPTER 6
Optimize Your Operations

F.R.E.E.D.O.M. Pillar Six

A business that depends entirely on you is not an asset. It is a job.

You built this business to give yourself freedom. So why does it feel like a cage?

You are the one who answers emails at midnight. The one who reviews every deliverable before it goes out. The one who handles the client emergency on a Saturday afternoon while your family waits in the car. You are the strategist, the salesperson, the quality control department, and the janitor. You are the first one to log in and the last one to log off. And somewhere in the back of your mind, a voice whispers the truth you have been avoiding: if you stopped working for two weeks, the whole thing would collapse.

That is not a business. That is a beautifully decorated trap.

You did not do this on purpose. It happened gradually. You hired help, but you never trained them to operate without your oversight. You built processes, but they live in your head instead of on paper. You delegated tasks, but you never delegated decisions. And now you are standing in the middle of a company that cannot breathe without your lungs.

This chapter is about building a business that can operate, deliver, and grow without your hands on every lever. Not so that you can walk away from it. So you can finally walk inside it as a CEO instead of an employee.

Your most valuable resource is not your revenue. It is your time.

Every hour you spend on a task that someone else could do is an hour you cannot spend on the work that only you can do. Strategy. Vision. Relationships. Growth. The things that actually move your business forward do not happen in your inbox at eleven o'clock at night. They happen when you have the space and the clarity to think like the CEO you are.

Optimizing your operations is not about becoming a cold, detached manager who never touches the work. It is about building systems that uphold the standard you have set, so the business can deliver your level of quality without depending on your personal effort for every single output.

The most successful businesses in the world are not run by people who do everything. They are run by people who build systems that do everything, and then protect those systems with discipline and intention. That is the shift this chapter is asking you to make. Not less care. Better infrastructure for the care you already give.

Emma's Story:
The Vacation That Proved the Problem

Emma was supposed to be in Cabo.

She had booked the trip three months in advance. She had told her team she would be offline for five days. She had set up an out-of-office message. She had told her husband that this was the trip where she would finally disconnect.

By day two, she was sitting on the hotel balcony with her laptop open, fielding Slack messages from her project manager, rewriting a client proposal her associate had drafted, and putting out a fire with a vendor who had missed a deadline. Her husband sat on the other side of the balcony, reading a novel, no longer bothering to ask if she was done.

"It was humiliating," she told me the week after she returned. "Not because my team did anything wrong. Because I never built a system that allowed them to do it right without me. Every process in my company lives in my head. Every decision runs through me. I told them I'd be offline, and then I proved that the business literally cannot function unless I'm sitting there watching it."

I asked her a question I had been waiting to ask for months.

"Emma, if someone wanted to buy your business today, could they? Could they walk in, look at your operations, and see a company that runs without you?"

The silence told me everything.

"No," she said finally. "They'd be buying me. And I'm exhausted."

That was the turning point. Emma did not need to work harder. She did not need to hire more people. She needed to build a machine. A set of documented processes, clear roles, consistent rhythms, and decision-making frameworks that allowed her team to operate at her standard without requiring her presence at every step.

She needed to stop being the engine and start being the CEO.

The Strategy: From Operator to CEO

There is a principle I share with every client who reaches this stage: you should not be the answer to every question in your business. You should be the person who builds the system that answers the questions.

Here is the framework for making that shift.

Step One: Conduct a Time Audit

Before you can optimize, you need to see where your time is actually going. For one week, track every task you perform in your business and how long it takes. Be honest. Include the emails, the Slack messages, the quick reviews, the five-minute fires that somehow eat an hour.

At the end of the week, sort your tasks into three categories.

CEO-Only Work. These are the tasks that require your unique expertise, relationships, or decision-making authority. Strategy development. Key client relationships. Financial oversight. Vision setting. These are the things that only you can do, and they should occupy the majority of your working hours.

Skilled Work. These are tasks that require talent and judgment but do not require you specifically. Writing proposals. Managing projects. Handling client communications. Quality review. These can be performed by a trained team member who understands your standards.

Administrative Work. These are the tasks that keep the wheels turning but do not require specialized skill. Scheduling. Data entry. Invoice processing. File organization. Email triage. These should be delegated immediately, either to a team member or a virtual assistant.

Most women entrepreneurs discover that they are spending sixty to seventy percent of their time on skilled and administrative work that someone else could be doing. That is not a failure of delegation. It is the absence of systems that make delegation possible.

Step Two: Document Your Processes

The single most powerful operational tool in your business is a standard operating procedure. It does not need to be elaborate. It does not need to be a hundred pages long. It needs to be a clear, step-by-step document that anyone on your team can follow to produce the same result you would produce if you did it yourself.

Start with the three tasks you repeat most often. Client onboarding. Proposal creation. Weekly reporting. Invoice processing. Whatever happens every week, document it. Write down every step, every decision point, every quality check. Include screenshots if it helps. Include the language you use in client-facing communications if tone matters.

Here is the discipline that makes this work: the first time a team member follows the process and has a question you did not anticipate, add the answer to the document. Every question is a gap in the system. Every gap you close makes the system stronger. Over time, the document becomes smarter than any training session you could deliver, because it holds the accumulated wisdom of every situation your team has faced.

Step Three: Establish a Weekly Operating Rhythm

Chaos in a business is often not caused by a lack of effort. It is caused by a lack of rhythm. When there is no consistent cadence for communication, review, and decision-making, everything becomes urgent and nothing gets resolved.

I recommend a simple weekly rhythm built around three touchpoints. The first is a Monday alignment meeting. Fifteen minutes. Every team member states what they are working on this week, what obstacles they face, and what they need from someone else to move forward. The second is a Wednesday check-in. This can be asynchronous, a quick Slack message or shared update confirming the week is on track. The third is a Friday close-out. Each person reports what was completed, what carries over, and what they learned.

This rhythm creates visibility without micromanagement. It surfaces problems before they become emergencies. And it gives you, the CEO, a clear view of your business that does not require you to be involved in every task to know what is happening.

Over time, the rhythm also builds trust. When your team consistently communicates what they are doing, what they have completed, and where they need support, you begin to see that they can carry the work. That evidence allows you to step back from the tasks and step into the strategy. You cannot trust what you cannot see, and the rhythm makes everything visible.

Step Four: Buy Back Your Time

Every task in your business has a cost. Not just the dollar cost of paying someone to do it, but the opportunity cost of you doing it instead of something more valuable.

Calculate your effective hourly rate. Take your annual owner's pay and divide it by the number of hours you work per year. If you are paying yourself one hundred fifty thousand dollars and working two thousand hours, your hourly rate is seventy-five dollars. Every task you perform that could be done by someone earning twenty-five dollars per hour is costing you fifty dollars in lost opportunity every single hour. I highly recommend reading Dan Martell's book *Buy Back Your Time* for full details of this concept.

The goal is not to eliminate all work from your plate. The goal is to protect your time for the work that generates the highest return. Delegate everything that falls below your effective hourly rate. Hire for the gaps. Automate what can be automated. And guard the hours that remain for the work that only you can do. Your time is the one resource you cannot manufacture more of. Treat it like the irreplaceable asset it is.

Your Operations Optimization Checklist

Use this checklist to assess the operational health of your business. Every unchecked box is a system waiting to be built.

- I have completed a one-week audit and categorized my tasks into CEO-Only, Skilled, and Administrative.

- I have identified the top three tasks I repeat most often that could be documented and delegated.
- I have created at least one standard operating procedure for a core, repeatable process.
- My team has access to documented processes and can follow them without my direct involvement.
- I have established a weekly operating rhythm with consistent touchpoints for alignment, check-ins, and close-outs.
- I know my effective hourly rate, and I use it to evaluate whether a task belongs on my plate.
- I have delegated or outsourced at least one administrative task that was consuming my CEO hours.
- My business can function for at least one full week without my direct involvement in daily operations.
- I have a clear organizational chart, even if the team is small, that defines who owns what.
- I spend at least fifty percent of my working hours on CEO-only work: strategy, vision, key relationships, and growth.

Your Tool: The CEO Time Audit and Process Map

This worksheet is designed in two parts that work sequentially.

Part One: The CEO Time Audit

This is a five-day tracking sheet. Each day, you log your tasks in thirty-minute blocks. At the end of the week, you color-code each block: green for CEO-only work, yellow for Skilled work, and red for Administrative work. Then you calculate the percentage of your week spent in each category.

Most clients expect to see mostly green. What they actually see is a week dominated by yellow and red. That visual shock is often the catalyst for real change. You cannot optimize what you cannot see, and this audit makes the invisible visible.

The target is to shift your week toward sixty percent or more CEO-only work within ninety days. You will not get there overnight. But every process you document and every task you delegate moves the needle closer.

Part Two: The Process Map

The second page is a template for documenting a single process. It includes fields for the process name, the trigger that initiates it, the step-by-step instructions, the quality checks at each stage, the expected outcome, and the person responsible for each step.

You will use this template repeatedly. Start with one process per week. By the end of a quarter, you will have twelve or more documented processes. By the end of six months, your business will have an operations manual that allows anyone on your team to deliver at your standard without asking you how.

Scripts and Templates

Script 1: The Delegation Conversation

When you are ready to hand a process over to a team member, use this language. It builds ownership instead of dependence.

"I've documented the process for [task name], and I want you to own it going forward. Here is the step-by-step guide. Follow it exactly the first three times. After that, if you see a way to improve it, bring me your suggestions. I trust you to run this, and I'm handing it to you because I believe you can deliver it at the standard our clients expect."

Script 2: The Weekly Rhythm Kickoff

Use this language to introduce your new meeting cadence to your team.

"Starting this week, we are running a simple weekly rhythm. On Mondays, we align on priorities. Wednesdays we check in. On Fridays, we close out. Each meeting will be short and focused. The goal is for all of us to know what is happening without anyone needing to chase updates. This is how we operate like a team that trusts each other enough to communicate consistently."

Script 3: The Operations Affirmation

Say this on Monday morning before your alignment meeting. Let it reset your relationship with your role.

"I am the CEO of this business, not the engine.

My systems hold the standard. My team delivers the work.

I lead by designing, not by doing everything myself."

Emma's Shift

Emma completed her time audit the first week. The results were sobering. Seventy-two percent of her week was yellow and red. She was spending the vast majority of her time on tasks that did not require her expertise. Client communications her project manager could handle. Proposal formatting her associate could own. Invoice follow-ups that a virtual assistant could manage without breaking a sweat.

She documented her three most repeated processes over the next ten days: client onboarding, proposal creation, and weekly reporting. She handed each one to a team member with the delegation script and the documented guide. She introduced the weekly rhythm at her next Monday meeting.

The before and after was measured in hours and in presence. Before the operations work, Emma worked an average of fifty-five hours per week, spent over seventy percent of her time on non-CEO tasks, and had not taken a full day off without checking her phone in over a year. Her team waited for her approval on nearly every decision. She was the answer to every question in her company.

After sixty days, her weekly hours dropped to forty-two. Her CEO-only percentage climbed to fifty-eight percent. Her team was running client onboarding, proposal delivery, and weekly reporting without her involvement. She took a long weekend with her family and did not open her laptop once.

She called me the Monday after she returned.

"The business ran, Sheena. It actually ran. No emergencies. No fires. My project manager handled a client issue I would normally have jumped on, and she handled it better than I would have. I sat on a beach and felt nothing but peace. That has never happened before."

I smiled. "That is what it feels like to own a business instead of being owned by one."

The Identity Shift

The woman who does everything herself and the woman who builds systems that do it for her are not separated by team size or budget. They are separated by a belief. The belief that your business can hold your standard without your hands on every piece of it.

That belief is not built by reading about it. It is built by documenting one process, delegating one task, and watching your team deliver without you. Then doing it again. And again. Until the evidence overwhelms the fear.

You have fortified your foundation, reduced your taxes, expanded your wealth, elevated your lifestyle, and designed your legacy. Every one of those pillars was built by you. But the business that supports all of it cannot keep running on your effort alone. It needs systems. It needs rhythm. It needs the infrastructure to deliver your vision without consuming your life.

You are no longer just the hardest worker in the room. You are the CEO of a business that works as hard as you do, even when you are not in the room at all.

Your operations are optimized. And the final chapter is where all of it comes together.

Because the final pillar is not about starting over. It is about scaling everything you have already built.

THE *AM I READY?* BASELINE ASSESSMENT

Score yourself across all seven F.R.E.E.D.O.M. pillars.

Find out where you stand and what to focus on next.

THE "AM I READY?" BASELINE ASSESSMENT

Score yourself across all seven F.R.E.E.D.O.M. pillars.
Find out where you stand and what to focus on next.

shebuildswealthy.com/assessment

CHAPTER 7
Multiply Your Money and Momentum

F.R.E.E.D.O.M. Pillar Seven

You have been placing green houses on every property. Now it is time to trade them in for the red hotel.

Do you remember the first time you played Monopoly?

Not the strategy part. The feeling part. The moment you realized that the game changed completely once you stopped buying individual properties and started building on the ones you already owned. One house. Then two. Then three. And then the moment that shifted everything: trading in the green houses for a red hotel.

That hotel did not appear out of nowhere. It was built, house by house, on a foundation that was already in place. You could not skip to it. You could not buy it on your first trip around the board. You had to pass GO. You had to collect your resources. You had to invest wisely, strategically, and patiently. And when the time came, the multiplication was not a gamble. It was the inevitable result of every small, intentional decision that had come before it.

I do not use this metaphor lightly. In my family, the red hotel is not a metaphor at all. My parents bought one, a real boutique hotel, after decades of building. I have stood in its lobby. I have checked in guests. I have cleaned the rooms. The board game is true.

That is where you are right now.

You have passed GO. You have collected your resources. You have laid green houses on every property in your financial life. Your foundation is solid. Your taxes are managed. Your wealth is growing. Your lifestyle is aligned. Your legacy is designed. Your operations are running. And now, standing at the final pillar, you are ready for the multiplication that all of it was building toward.

This chapter is not about starting something new. It is about scaling everything you have already built. It is about turning six solid pillars into a compound engine that generates momentum on its own. It is the red hotel.

Multiplication is not addition. Addition is doing more of the same. Working more hours. Taking on more clients. Launching another offer. That is linear growth, and it has a ceiling. The ceiling is you.

Multiplication is different. Multiplication happens when the systems you have built start compounding against each other. When your tax savings fund your wealth account, which grows on its own, which funds your lifestyle without requiring more revenue, which frees your time, which allows you to build better systems, which create more profit, which feeds the cycle again. That is not a ladder. That is a flywheel. And once it starts spinning, it does not need you to push it harder. It needs you to protect it and let it run.

Most women entrepreneurs stall at addition. They believe the only way to grow is to do more. This chapter teaches you to grow by leveraging what you have already done. Every pillar you have built is a multiplier. This chapter is where you connect them and watch the compounding begin.

Emma's Story: The Morning She Stopped Hustling

It was a Thursday morning in October. Emma sat at her kitchen table with a cup of coffee, her laptop closed for the first time during working hours in as long as she could remember. Her phone was in the other room. The house was quiet. Lily was at school. The business was running.

She was not working. She was thinking.

Not scrambling. Not reacting. Not putting out a fire or chasing a deadline. Thinking. Strategically, clearly, and with a calm she had not felt since the early days of her business, back when the stakes were small enough that she could breathe between decisions.

On the notepad in front of her, she had written a single question in black ink:

"What would I build if I was not afraid of losing what I already have?"

A year ago, that question would have paralyzed her. A year ago, she was sitting on her bedroom floor surrounded by unopened envelopes, terrified of her own bank account. A year ago, she could not name her monthly revenue, her tax rate, her net worth, or her cash runway without spiraling into shame.

Now she could name all four without looking them up.

She picked up her pen and started writing. Not a to-do list. Not a client proposal. A vision. For the first time, she was not building from fear. She was building from abundance. She had a foundation that could hold weight. She had a tax strategy that kept more in her pocket. She had a wealth account that was compounding. She had a lifestyle she enjoyed without guilt. She had a legacy plan that would protect her family. She had a team that could run the business without her sitting in the room.

She called me that afternoon.

"Sheena, I want to open a second revenue stream. Not because I'm desperate. Because I finally have the infrastructure to support it. I'm thinking about a group coaching program. My one-on-one clients keep asking me to teach what I know, and I think I'm ready. My team can handle the operations. My finances can absorb the startup costs. And I actually have the time to build it because I'm not drowning in the day-to-day anymore."

I paused for a moment, not because I was surprised, but because I wanted her to hear what she had just said. Every sentence she spoke contained a pillar. Infrastructure. Team. Finances. Time. She was not guessing. She was not hoping. She was ready, and the readiness was built, not borrowed.

"Emma," I said, "that is not hustle. That is multiplication. You are not working harder. You are leveraging everything you have already built. That is the red hotel."

The Strategy: The Multiplication Engine

Multiplication is not a single strategy. It is the result of all six previous pillars working together. But there are specific actions you can take in this final phase to accelerate the compounding and ensure that your growth is sustainable, not just exciting.

Step One: Identify Your Highest-Leverage Opportunity

Not every growth opportunity is a multiplication opportunity. Some are just more work disguised as progress. The key question is: does this opportunity leverage the systems, the assets, or the audience I have already built?

A second revenue stream that uses your existing team, your existing expertise, and your existing client relationships is multiplication. A brand-new business in an unrelated industry that requires new skills, a new audience, and a new team is an addition. Both can be valuable. But only one of them compounds what you have already built.

Before you pursue any new growth initiative, run it through a simple filter. Can my current team support it? Does it align with my existing expertise? Can it be delivered using the systems I have already documented? Will it increase revenue without proportionally increasing my personal time investment? If the answer to most of those questions is yes, you have found a multiplier.

Step Two: Diversify Your Income Streams

A business with only one revenue stream is a business standing on one leg. It may balance for a while, but it is always one disruption away from falling.

The most resilient businesses have multiple streams that feed from the same source. If you are a consultant, you can add a group program. If you run a service business, you can create a digital product or a course. If you own a physical business, you can license your model or offer a membership. If you have intellectual property, you can package it for passive delivery.

Diversification does not mean doing everything at once. It means choosing one additional stream that complements your core business, building it with the same intentional structure you applied to every other pillar, and letting it mature before you add another. The goal is not to have seven income streams by next quarter. The goal is to have two or three that are stable, profitable, and do not require your daily involvement to function.

Step Three: Reinvest Strategically

Every dollar your business generates has four possible destinations: it can pay your taxes, fund your lifestyle, grow your wealth, or be reinvested into the business. You have already built systems for the first three. This step is about being intentional with the fourth.

Strategic reinvestment means putting money back into the areas of your business that generate the highest return. That might be hiring a key team member who frees twenty hours of your week. It might be investing in a marketing system that generates leads while you sleep. It might be upgrading your technology to automate a process that currently requires manual effort. It might be a professional development investment in yourself that opens a new tier of clients or a new pricing level.

The discipline is in the word strategic. Reinvestment without intention is just spending. Reinvestment with a clear expected return is multiplication.

Step Four: Protect the Flywheel

The most dangerous moment for a growing business is not the struggle phase. It is the momentum phase. When things are working, when revenue is climbing, when new opportunities are appearing, the temptation is to say yes to everything. To add. To expand. To chase the next shiny thing because you finally have the resources to do it.

That is where discipline matters most. The flywheel you have built, the compounding engine of foundation, tax strategy, wealth, lifestyle, legacy, and operations, only works if you protect it. Every yes that does not serve the system is a drag on the wheel. Every distraction that pulls you back into operator mode instead of CEO mode is friction.

Your job in this phase is not to do more. It is to do fewer things with greater impact. To say no to opportunities that look exciting but do not multiply what you have built. To guard your time, your systems, and your focus the way you guard your wealth account. With intention. With boundaries. With the confidence of a woman who knows that what she has already built is powerful enough to compound on its own.

Your Multiplication Checklist

Use this checklist to assess your readiness for multiplication. Every unchecked box is a foundation to strengthen before you scale.

- All six previous F.R.E.E.D.O.M. pillars are actively implemented (foundation, tax, wealth, lifestyle, legacy, operations).

- I have identified at least one high-leverage growth opportunity that uses my existing team, expertise, and systems.
- I have evaluated potential new revenue streams and selected one to build intentionally.
- My current business can sustain a new initiative without requiring me to return to operator-level involvement.
- I have a reinvestment budget that is separate from my operating expenses, tax reserves, and wealth transfers.
- I have a clear expected return for every dollar I reinvest into my business.
- I have a system for saying no to opportunities that do not multiply what I have already built.
- My flywheel is protected: I am spending most of my time on strategy and high-leverage activities, not on daily operations.
- I review my F.R.E.E.D.O.M. framework quarterly to ensure all seven pillars are functioning and current.
- I have a vision for the next three years that is grounded in multiplication, not just addition.

Your Tool: The F.R.E.E.D.O.M. Flywheel Review

This is the only worksheet in the book that is used forever.

The F.R.E.E.D.O.M. Flywheel Review is a one-page quarterly assessment. It lists all seven pillars of the framework. For each pillar, you answer two questions. First: is this pillar currently active and functioning? Second: what is the one action I can take this quarter to strengthen it?

The review also includes a section at the bottom called *The Multiplication Question*. It asks:

What is the single highest-leverage action I can take this quarter that compounds the work I have already done?

That question keeps your focus sharp. It prevents you from chasing new projects when the current ones need attention. It reminds you that growth is not always about building something new. Sometimes the highest-leverage action is strengthening what you have already built.

Complete this review on the first day of every quarter. Tape it to your wall next to your Dream Funding Plan from Chapter 3. Over time, these reviews will tell the story of a woman who built something extraordinary, not in a single sprint, but in a steady, intentional rhythm of fortifying, reducing, expanding, elevating, designing, optimizing, and multiplying.

Scripts and Templates

Script 1: The Multiplication Filter

Before you say yes to any new opportunity, run it through these five questions. If you cannot answer yes to at least four of them, it is not a multiplier. It is a distraction.

Does this leverage my existing expertise, audience, or relationships?

Can my current team support this without adding significant overhead?

Will this generate revenue without proportionally increasing my personal time?

Does this align with my three-year vision and my F.R.E.E.D.O.M. framework?

Can I build this using the systems and processes I already have documented?

Script 2: The Quarterly Vision Reset

Use this language with yourself at the start of every quarter. Write it in the front of your planner or journal.

"This quarter, I am not chasing new business. I am compounding what I have already built. I will strengthen one pillar, multiply one asset, and protect the flywheel. Growth does not require urgency. It requires intention."

Script 3: The Final Affirmation

This is the affirmation that holds all seven pillars together. Say it on the first day of every quarter, after completing your Flywheel Review.

"My foundation is fortified. My taxes are managed.

My wealth is expanding. My lifestyle is aligned.

My legacy is designed. My operations are running.

And my momentum is multiplying.

I am not just keeping more cash. I am building F.R.E.E.D.O.M."

Emma's Shift

Emma launched her group coaching program four months after that Thursday morning at the kitchen table. She built it using her existing content, her existing systems, and her existing team. Her project manager handled the operations. Her associate managed client communications. Emma designed the curriculum, facilitated the sessions, and showed up as the expert she had always been, only now she had the infrastructure to serve more people without burning out.

The before and after told the full story of her year. When Emma first called my office, she was sitting on her bedroom floor with a stack of unopened envelopes and a shame spiral that kept her from looking at her own bank account. Her business was earning revenue but building nothing. She had no financial foundation, no tax strategy, no wealth system, no aligned lifestyle, no legacy plan, no operational structure, and no path to multiplication.

Twelve months later, her accounts were consolidated and purposeful. Her tax bill had dropped by over fifteen thousand dollars. Her wealth account was funded and compounding. She was paying herself consistently and spending with intention through her Joy Budget. Her will, trust, and legacy letter were signed and stored. Her team was running daily operations without her involvement. And she had launched a second revenue stream that was generating income while she was hiking a trail, reading to her daughter, or sitting in silence with a cup of coffee and a closed laptop.

She sent me a text on the anniversary of her first call. It was short.

"I started this year on the floor. I'm ending it as a woman who owns her money, her time, and her life. Thank you for showing me the board, Sheena. I'm not just passing GO anymore. I'm building the red hotel."

The Identity Shift

You started this book as a woman who was working hard and wondering where all the money was going. You are finishing it as a woman who knows exactly where her money goes, because she is the one directing it.

You have fortified your foundation. You have reduced your lifetime tax bill. You have expanded your wealth. You have elevated your lifestyle. You have designed your legacy. You have optimized your operations. And now you have multiplied your money and your momentum into a flywheel that compounds everything you have built.

You are not the same woman who picked up this book. Not because you learned a few tricks. Because you changed the way you see yourself in relation to money. You stopped being the woman who avoids, who guesses, and who hopes it works out. You became the woman who looks, who plans, who decides, and who builds.

That is F.R.E.E.D.O.M. Not a fantasy. Not a slogan. A framework you installed into your life, one pillar at a time, until it became the structure your entire future stands on.

The board is yours now. The houses are green. The hotel is red. And every move you make from here is a move you make with clarity, confidence, and the quiet power of a woman who finally knows what she is worth.

Keep more cash. Build more wealth. Live more freely.

You have earned this. Every single piece of it.

You have completed the F.R.E.E.D.O.M. Framework.

Every worksheet referenced in this book is waiting for you, free and fillable, at shebuildswealthy.com/toolkit.

Acknowledgments

This book exists because of the women who trusted me with their numbers, their fears, and their dreams before any of this was written.

To my clients, past and present: you taught me everything I know about courage. You sat across from me with trembling hands and open hearts, and you let me see behind the curtain. Every framework in this book was forged in the fire of your real lives. I do not take that trust lightly, and I never will.

To my mother, who ran a daycare out of our living room and taught me that entrepreneurship does not require a corner office to be real. You showed me what it looks like to build something from nothing, to serve with your whole heart, and to make a dollar stretch further than anyone thought possible. Every word in this book is rooted in the soil you tilled that got you to your red hotel.

To my stepdad: you came into my life when I was sixteen and chose to stay. You became the steady partner my mother deserved after all those years of holding everything alone. And then the two of you went and did the thing this entire book is reaching for. You bought the hotel. A real one. Every time I tell a woman to build toward her red hotel, I am telling her something I have watched come true at my own family's table. Thank you for being the kind of support that lets someone else's dream land.

To my husband: we stood in the wreckage together, and you never once let go of my hand. You believed in the rebuild before there was a single piece of evidence that it would work. This framework was forged in a fire we walked through side by side, and every page of it carries your steadiness. Thank you for choosing the foundation with me.

To my team at *She Builds Wealthy Co/Growth Advisors & Tax Consultants,* who have helped me put this framework into practice one day at a time.

To every woman who picked up this book because she was tired of being confused, ashamed, or afraid of her own money: you are the reason I wrote it. You are not broken. You were never broken. You simply needed a framework that met you where you were and showed you the way forward.

This book is for you. All of it.

With love and intention,

Sheena

About the Author

Sheena Jones is a Certified Public Accountant, tax strategist, financial educator, and founder of Growth Advisors & Tax Consultants and She Builds Wealthy Co. As the creator of the F.R.E.E.D.O.M. Framework, she helps women business owners keep more of what they earn, build lasting wealth, and create financial freedom through practical tax strategies and intentional financial planning.

Sheena's path to financial expertise was not a straight line. She grew up watching her mother run a daycare business from their living room, learning early that women could build empires from the spaces they already occupied. She went on to build a career in public accounting, working at one of the Big 4 firms in

Chicago, where she mastered the technical side of tax strategy and financial planning at the highest level.

But it was the seasons of personal loss and rebuilding that transformed her approach. A business betrayal nearly cost Sheena and her husband everything they had built. The long, deliberate work of starting over taught her that financial mastery was not just about the numbers. It was about identity, safety, and the belief that every woman deserves to feel powerful in her own financial life.

Today, Sheena works with women entrepreneurs across the country through her CPA Firm, *Growth Advisors & Tax Consultants* and her educational business, *She Builds Wealthy Co*, offering tax strategy, wealth planning, and the kind of CFO-level partnership that most small business owners never knew they could access. Her mission is to end financial illiteracy for women entrepreneurs and to prove that wealth is not about hustle. It is about structure, strategy, and the courage to look at your numbers and decide what they mean.

Sheena lives with her husband, whose steadiness through the hardest season of her life is her proof that the framework holds in love as well as in money. Sheena believes that wealth is more than a bank balance. Wealth is safety in your body, confidence in your business, and freedom in your life.

She lives this work every day. And she wrote this book so you can, too.

Connect with Sheena

shebuildswealthy.com

hello@email.shebuildswealthy.com

@sheenajonescpa

Recommended Resources

The following resources are tools and references I recommend to clients. They are not required to implement the *F.R.E.E.D.O.M. Framework*, but they may deepen your understanding and support your journey.

Books

Profit First by Mike Michalowicz. A practical system for ensuring your business is profitable from day one. Pairs well with Chapters 1 and 3.

Buy Back Your Time by Dan Martell. A guide to freeing yourself from the day-to-day so you can focus on what matters most. Essential reading alongside Chapter 6.

We Should All Be Millionaires by Rachel Rodgers. A wealth-building manifesto for women that aligns with the identity work throughout this book.

Traction by Gino Wickman. The Entrepreneurial Operating System for building a business that runs on vision, people, and process. Foundational to Chapter 6.

The Psychology of Money by Morgan Housel. A beautiful exploration of how our emotions, habits, and histories shape our financial decisions. Pairs with every chapter.

Financial Tools and Software

QuickBooks Online or *Xero.* Cloud-based bookkeeping platforms for tracking revenue, expenses, and profit in real time.

Relay or *Novo.* Business banking platforms designed for entrepreneurs, with easy sub-account creation for your three-account structure.

MileIQ or *Everlance.* Automated mileage tracking apps for documenting business vehicle use.

Empower (formerly Personal Capital) or *Monarch Money.* Net worth and wealth tracking tools that give you a single-dashboard view of your financial life.

Professional Support

The frameworks in this book are designed to be implemented with or without professional help. However, I strongly recommend that every woman entrepreneur build relationships with the following professionals as her business grows.

A CPA or Tax Strategist who offers proactive planning, not just annual filing. Ask the questions in Chapter 2.

An Estate Attorney who specializes in small business owners and can help you build the legacy architecture from Chapter 5.

A Fee-Only Financial Advisor who is a fiduciary, meaning they are legally required to act in your best interest. Avoid advisors who earn commissions on the products they recommend.

A Bookkeeper who provides monthly reports you can understand and who will walk you through the numbers, not just send them.

Work with Sheena

If this book lit something inside you and you want to go deeper, I would love to work with you.

Growth Advisors & Tax Consultants

Growth Advisors & Tax Consultants offers tax strategy, wealth planning, and fractional CFO services for women entrepreneurs who are ready to stop guessing and start building with a partner in their corner. Whether you are implementing the *F.R.E.E.D.O.M. Framework* for the first time or scaling what you have already built, our team meets you where you are.

The F.R.E.E.D.O.M. Intensive

A focused, one-on-one engagement where we walk through all seven pillars of the framework together, customized to your specific business, income level, and goals. This is the accelerated version of everything in this book, tailored to your numbers and your life.

Speaking and Workshops

I speak at conferences, corporate events, and women's organizations on the topics of tax strategy, wealth building, and financial identity for women entrepreneurs. If your organization would benefit from the F.R.E.E.D.O.M. message, I would be honored to bring it to your stage.

Stay Connected

For updates, resources, bonus content, and community, visit:

shebuildswealthy.com

hello@email.shebuildswealthy.com

@sheenajonescpa

I read every message. I see every woman who raises her hand and says, "I'm ready." And I am here when you are.

YOUR NEXT STEP

You finished Keep More Cash.

Now let us build your F.R.E.E.D.O.M. together.

shebuildswealthy.com/freedom

Keep More Cash.

Build More Wealth.

Live More Freely.

The F.R.E.E.D.O.M. Framework

by Sheena Jones, CPA

www.ingramcontent.com/pod-product-compliance
Lightning Source LLC
LaVergne TN
LVHW050822061126
851857LV00012B/929
9798950701085